the breakbeat bible

BY MIKE ADAMO

Editor: Joe Bergamini
Layout Design: Rich Collins
Cover Design: Rich Collins
Engraving: Willie Rose
Executive Producer: Mike Adamo

Catalog: HL06620153
ISBN: 1423496337

Audio credits:

Engineer/ Mix/ Master:
Nicholas Buford

Instrumental tracks created by:
Paper.Beatz.Rock

Paper.Beatz.Rock is: Remshot (Jeremy de la Cruz), also of 17 Hertz, and Brod Rob

To Download Audio for this Book:
Go To: halleonard.com/mylibrary
Enter Code: 1003-1212-4352-5167

A DIVISION OF HUDSON MUSIC, LLC.

www.hudsonmusic.com • www.thebreakbeatbible.com

The Breakbeat Bible
Table of Contents

Foreword
There's something inherently kinetic about a drum break.

Maybe it's the drummer's intent to play the absolute tightest, funkiest, most revolutionary beat possible. Maybe it's the vibe of the studio session. Whatever it is, the inherent energy of the break carries over to the music that uses the break as a sample. As I began to analyze drum breaks used in hip-hop, I realized that authentically replicating them on the drumset is more difficult than it seems. The exercises, beats, concepts, and transcriptions in this book are things that I've been developing over the past several years. My intention has been to tighten up and take my own playing to the next level. I hope this book will help other players as much as it has been helping me. I also hope it brings as much enjoyment to drummers as other books have brought to me over the years. After all, that's what it's all about.

Mike Adamo

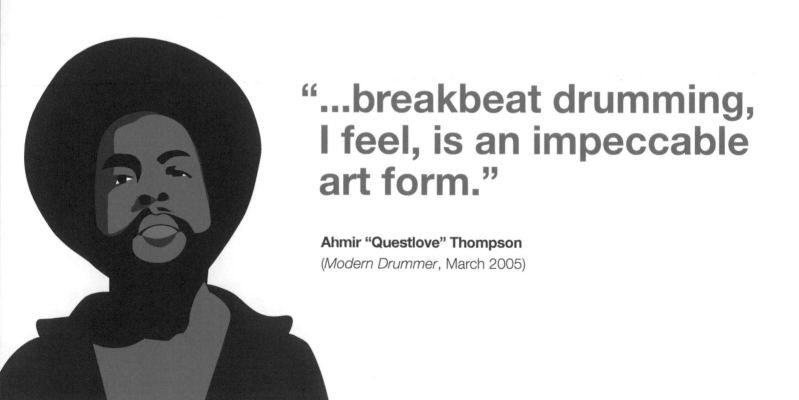

"...breakbeat drumming, I feel, is an impeccable art form."

Ahmir "Questlove" Thompson
(*Modern Drummer*, March 2005)

What is a Breakbeat?

It's the summer of 1975. You're walking through the heart of the South Bronx, NYC. Suddenly, a dude pulls a knife on you and wants to jack your wallet. You cut into an alley and lose him after a quick chase. You stop running. In the distance you hear the rumble of a nasty funk track played through a huge sound system. As you follow the vibrations, the music gets louder. You turn a corner and walk up on a huge block party in full effect. Gritty funk is blasting through the biggest sound system you've ever heard or seen. Then, everything in the song cuts out except for the drums. Everyone at the party flips out. Kids proceed to bust out the most incredible dance moves you've ever seen in your life. You're witnessing the dawn of one of the largest global cultural movements this planet has ever seen.

The DJ was most likely Kool Herc, and those dancers were some of the original break dancers. As DJ Kool Herc spun records at those block parties, he realized that kids busted out their best dance moves during the drum breaks (when all other instruments stop playing except the drums). Herc began setting up two turntables next to each other and having the same record play on both. He would cue up the drum break, so when it ended on one record, he would switch the cross-fader to the other turntable, where the beginning of the same break was waiting to be played. Repeating this process between the two turntables, he was able to extend the drum break for as long as he wanted. It should also be noted that around this same time, also in the Bronx, another DJ named Grandmaster Flash was cultivating this same technique. This new technique allowed the people to dance harder and longer, which elevated the vibe of the party. This was the beginning of break dancing. The Rock Steady Crew is probably the most famous break dance crew, and Crazy Legs and Frosty Freeze are some of the most legendary break dancers to emerge from that era. With breakbeats as a foundation, hip-hop was born.

In the postmodern digital age, a breakbeat is what producers sample and make into drum loops. The breaks usually come from old-school funk and soul records, but can be harvested from any genre. The sampling process developed into modern musical genres such as hip-hop, Drum'n'Bass, and Jungle. Music, drumming, and the world would never be the same. There's a common misconception regarding the term "breakbeat." It's often used as a synonym to describe the up-tempo, hyper-syncopated beats used in electronic music styles such as Drum'n'Bass and Jungle. (This is because these styles do not have the constant "four-on-the-floor" kick drum pattern of Trance and House. The beats are "broken up" and syncopated with sixteenth-note subdivisions.) While this is true, it's also limiting. Breakbeat music is rooted in the sampling of drum breaks, or the programmed imitation of these sampled beats. Therefore, the term is used when describing the drum style for a variety of modern musical genres.

Here's a list of some genres that fall under the breakbeat umbrella, and a brief description.

Big Beat: The beats of this genre are generated with individual sampled drum sounds, or from pre-existing beats that were slowed down or sped up. The beats are generally distorted, compressed, heavy, and have limited syncopation. Big Beat sometimes features synthesizer-generated loops and patterns. The tempos are generally in the 90-140 bpm range. Some artists that work in this genre are Fatboy Slim, The Crystal Method, The Chemical Brothers, and Bassnectar.

Acid Breaks: This genre is characterized by syncopated beats in conjunction with powerful, synthesized overtones and harmonies. Listeners of Acid Breaks often claim that the combination of beats, overtones, and harmonies creates trance-like, out-of-body experiences. The first Acid Break track, "Acid Break," was created by Zak Baney in 1987.

Breakbeat Hardcore: This genre mixes "four-on-the-floor" kick drum patterns with syncopated beats. It originated in the U.K. in the late '80s and early '90s. Breakbeat Hardcore artists utilize synthesizers, drum machines, keyboards, and samplers to create their music. Some artists that work in this genre are DJ Seduction, The Prodigy, and Wax Doctor.

Breakcore: This genre was developed in Germany and the U.K. in the mid '90s. It's characterized by complex, aggressively syncopated beats, unconventional song structures, melodic chord progressions, and sudden rhythmic shifts. Breakcore sometimes contains distorted samples of drum breaks paired with "darker-edged" musical influences. The beats occasionally feature a distorted Roland 909 kick drum sound. Breakcore artists use computers, keyboards, synthesizers, drum machines, and samplers to make their tracks. Contemporary Breakcore artists include Dark Matter Soundsystem and Drop the Lime.

Hardcore Breaks: This genre features looped and processed samples of breakbeats, heavy bass lines, melodic piano lines, acute synthesizer riffs, and vocal samples. The tracks fall in the 145-155 bpm range. Some of the more popular Hardcore Breaks artists include Darkus, DJ Sike, and Whizzkick.

Rave Breaks: This style has many of the same characteristics of Hardcore Breaks. However, songs in this genre are between 135 and 145 bpm. Junki Munki, Sy and Unknown, and Ratpack are some of the more popular Rave Breaks artists.

Jungle: This term is often used interchangeably with Drum'n'Bass. There is no universally accepted distinction between the two genres. However, in some circles Jungle is accepted as the prototype for Drum'n'Bass. It developed as a backlash to the increasing popularity of the rave scene. The early artists of this genre, such as DJ Fabio and DJ Grooverider, began increasing the tempo of rave music. In addition, they began adding more syncopated elements. In its early stages, artists used sped-up samples of classic breaks such as the "Amen" break, the "Apache" break, and the "Funky Drummer" break. The style is characterized by faster tempos in the 190-210 bpm range. The drums of this genre are frenetic, and feature syncopated beats with intricate 16th-note subdivisions.

Drum'n'Bass: This is one of the more popular genres under the breakbeat umbrella. The music of this genre is usually between 160 and 180 bpm. There is debate as to whether Drum'n'Bass and Jungle are the same thing. However, it's widely accepted that Drum'n'Bass evolved from Jungle, and they now co-exist as separate genres. Drum'n'Bass originated as producers wanted to move away from the criminal activity that began to associate with Jungle. As the genre developed, producers began programming the beats with sampled drum sounds. The drums of this style generally feature snare accents on beats two and four with varied kick drum and hi-hat patterns. These beats are not as syncopated as those of Jungle. In Drum'n'Bass, the bass line is in "half-time" in relation to the drums (80-90 bpm). Some of the more popular artists of this genre are Goldi, Diesel Boy, and Shapeshifter.

Broken Beat: This is a more "human" form of breakbeat music, containing elements of funk, soul, and hip-hop. Broken Beat is often considered to be more refined than other forms of dance music. The songs of this genre are usually in the 80-110 bpm range. Some contemporary artists of this genre are IG Culture and Break Science.

Hip-Hop: Songs in this genre are typically between 85 and 105 bpm (but can be slower or faster). The drums of this style are characterized by a heavy "two and four" snare pattern in conjunction with various kick and hi-hat patterns. Other instruments are added to the beats, either as samples or through live instrumentation. MCs then rhyme over the beats. Drum breaks are the lifeblood of hip-hop. The invention of drum machines enabled producers to imitate these breaks with a process known as beat programming. In addition to the music, the term "hip-hop" encompasses a larger culture including break dancing, graffiti, and knowledge.

The Mission of *The Breakbeat Bible*

This book focuses on the fundamentals of breakbeat drumming, as applied to hip-hop. However, you can also apply the grooves/concepts from the book to a variety of genres.

A breakbeat is, in essence, a funk beat. However, it's also much more. Due to the nature of looping, and the precision of programmed drum patterns, there's an impeccable tightness to a breakbeat beyond that of your average funk beat. This is not to say that one is better than the other; they're just different. For example, let's consider the song "Here Comes the Meter Man" by The Meters, from their 1969 self-titled release. Zigaboo Modeliste's drumming pushes and pulls throughout the track. The tempo pretty much stays the same, but if you analyzed the drum track in Beat Detective, the kick, snare, and hi-hat parts would fall in slightly different places in each measure. This is beautiful because it gives the song a unique feel and swing. This is funk drumming at its finest. In contrast, consider the Digable Planet's song "Black Ego" from the album *Blowout Comb* (Pendulum Records, 1994). The drum pattern from this song is based on a two-bar drum break sampled from Zig's playing at the end of "Here Comes the Meter Man." **It's a looped two-bar drum break, therefore, in "Black Ego" the timing nuances of the kick, snare, and hi-hat occur at the exact same place in each measure.** A certain precision comes from this looped drum pattern that doesn't from a drummer playing throughout an entire song. Programmed drum patterns are even more precise than looped breakbeat samples. They're created with computers and drum machines, and are inherently precise (unless you program by hand, in real time, with the quantization off, like Jay Dee a.k.a. J. Dilla sometimes did). Due to the prevalence of drum loops and programmed beats in contemporary music, in addition to the use of Pro Tools in post-production to fix the recorded playing of live drummers, people have come to expect a certain level of perfection in drum beats.

The Breakbeat Bible begins with the Elements section. Here, breakbeat drumming is divided into thirteen elements. Each element is introduced and discussed in its own chapter. The introduction and discussion are followed by exercises, beats, and eight-bar phrases pertaining to the specific element. These give drummers the opportunity to practice reproducing breakbeats on a drumset. The Elements section is followed by Beats With Everything, Beats With Drops, Fills, and Breakbeat Transcriptions. The next section of the book is the Click Track Loops. This section contains various click track patterns meant to be programmed with a drum machine. They're designed to strengthen the internal clock while enhancing your precision, timing, and groove. Practicing with these loops will bring a new degree of tightness to your drumming. They will give you the control necessary to reproduce breakbeats with loop-like precision. The Click Track Loop section also discusses various options for non-traditional metronome usage, should you not have a drum machine. These will also tighten up your drumming, although not quite to the degree of the full-on Click Track Loops. The final section of the book contains a brief overview of Dubstep.

Breakbeat drumming is an art form. There's a deeper level of tightness and accuracy that we're striving for here, and this book will help you to attain it.

These are important times, and music is playing a critical role in initiating change and promoting positivity. In a time when DJs and computers are taking over the music scene, it's important for drummers to step up in tightness and groove. This book will help drummers match beats and play with loops and DJs in a live context. After all, there is no greater blessing in music than the presence and soul of a drummer. Word up.

Concepts

There are three main concepts that should be used in conjunction with practicing the exercises and beats in this book.

The first is playing along with recorded songs. This will help you develop the feel of the type of music you want to learn. It'll also develop a stronger sense of time, your internal clock, and your groove. Use the following four-step process when practicing/playing along with songs:

1. Listen to the song a few times. Check out what the drummer is doing, and how this fits in with the other instruments. It'll help a lot if you actually transcribe (write out) the drum part.

2. Play along with the song 10 times in a row.

3. Record yourself playing along to the song (listen to the song through headphones, so just your playing is recorded).

4. Listen back to the recording and analyze your playing. If your beat doesn't sound and feel like the recording, figure out what's wrong and repeat the process. Keep on doing this until your playing begins to match the recording. Don't worry, you won't lose your individual feel by doing this. You will gain the control necessary to duplicate pre-existing feels and beats.

Also, practice the exercises and beats in this book along with music that you want to get the feel of. In other words, use recorded music as your click track. Obviously, the exercises and beats from this book will be different than the drum parts of the song. That's okay. This process is more about capturing and applying a certain feel to the exercises and beats. For example, use albums such as James Brown's *In the Jungle Groove* if you want to get that classic breakbeat feel, or use Gang Starr's *Moment of Truth* or A Tribe Called Quest's *Midnight Marauders* if you want to get that classic 1990s East Coast hip-hop feel. The more styles you do this with, the better off you'll be.

The second concept is playing along with a metronome/click track. This helps you develop the ability to play with metronomically tight time (if the situation requires it). It also gives you the ability to bend the time, play "in between the cracks" of straight and swung, or play slightly behind or slightly in front of the beat (without dragging or rushing the pulse). These are important skills to have for contemporary drumming.

At first, practice the exercises and beats of this book with a standard quarter note click track. When you're comfortable with this, you can begin practicing with the Click Track Loops (located on pg. 162). You don't necessarily have to finish the other sections of the book before getting into the Click Track Loops.

Play the exercises and beats in this book at various tempos. In order to build solid, feel-good grooves, start slow and gradually increase the tempo. A general tempo range for the exercises and beats is between 85 and 105 bpm (the average hip-hop tempo). However, you should be comfortable playing them slower and faster as well. A lot of the beats in this book will also work well in the Drum'n'Bass and Jungle tempo ranges (about 160-180 bpm and 190-210 bpm respectively). If you want to take them to that level, make sure you start slow and gradually increase the tempo. Otherwise, your playing will be strained, rushed, and uneven. If you're interested in Drum'n'Bass and Jungle, check out *Jungle/Drum'n'Bass for the Acoustic Drumset* (Alfred Publishing) by Johnny Rabb.

The third concept is feeling an underlying half-note or whole-note pulse as you practice/play various grooves (instead of feeling a quarter-, eighth-, or sixteenth-note pulse). This is important for generating a relaxed, open feel. Intense practice with a metronome, and/or the Click Track Loops, despite tightening up your playing, may cause your overall groove to become forced and rigid. Feeling the underlying half-note or whole-note pulse will give your playing a more open, relaxed feel, while maintaining the tightness developed with the metronome/Click Track Loops.

Using these concepts will greatly enhance your internal clock. They'll tighten up your playing and help you authentically replicate breakbeats on the drumset. They will also give you the skills to match programmed beats and perform with DJs, sequenced backing tracks, and loops.

Practice

It will take hours of practice/playing to take your drumming to the next level. It's up to you to decide how intensely you want to practice. Increased skill level is not something money can buy. Lessons with the best teachers and the best new gear in the world will not make you a better player without practice. You can't buy skills, and you can't use a computer to program yourself to be better (yet). That's the value of intense, focused practice. It's something you earn for yourself, and no one can take that away from you.

Listening

Once you attain a certain level of technical proficiency, things you hear in music will begin to automatically emerge in your playing. Therefore, it's important to listen to the style of music that you want to play. Although this book discusses artists that use breakbeats, it is by no means the final word on the topic. Hopefully this book will be a launch pad for your journey into the greater "Breakbeat Universe." It's also important to draw inspiration from a variety of musical styles. That way you'll always keep your playing fresh.

Drum Sounds

The drum sound for the breakbeat style is often very tight and controlled. In the studio this can be accomplished in a variety of ways. One technique of old-school soul music is to cover the entire drum set with a blanket. In addition to this, the drummer plays as lightly as possible. This creates a dirty, gritty, compressed sound. A controlled, dry drum sound makes it easier for engineers to add effects after the drums have been recorded. You can also achieve this type of drum sound by putting t-shirts over the drums, duct taping the drum head, or putting your wallet on the drum head. There's also a product called Moon Gel that works well.

The dimensions of the drum also play a big role. Drums that are smaller in depth and diameter tend to be tighter and more controlled. Also, woods such as poplar and birch tend to be more controlled than maple. There are a variety of heads designed to create a controlled sound as well. These are often vented or pre-dampened. Do some research and test out as many products as possible to find out what you like and what works best for your style.

Some breakbeats feature a bright, open sound. This can be achieved by tuning the drums to a medium-tight tension and letting them ring out. Tensioning the bottom head tighter than the top will further increase this effect, as will using heads that are not pre-dampened. Also, the metals (nickel, brass, steel, or titanium) used for some snare drums are generally brighter-sounding than wood. Play on as many different brands of drums as you can. Each company is a little different.

The sound of the breakbeat kick drum is usually big, open, and low-end heavy. Drummers often emulate the low-end kick sounds of drum machines, such as the Roland 808. This can be achieved with bigger kick drums. Experiment with different head options. Also, the Yamaha Sub-Kick and the AKG D112 microphone can enhance the low end of your kick drum sound. Another option is to use a triggering system on your kick drum. Triggering basically involves placing a sensor on your drum. When the drum is struck, in addition to hearing the acoustic sound of the drum, the sensor adds an electronic sampled sound. You can then trigger the kick drum to sound like any sample you want. However, the situation may sometimes call for a tighter kick sound. Experiment with pre-dampened kick drum heads, or with dampening the kick by placing blankets or towels inside the drum. Again, sometimes engineers want a dry, controlled kick sound (live or in the studio). This way, they can add effects.

Experiment with the different variables. You might find that you like a big, open kick, paired with a tight, controlled snare and dampened toms. Or, you might like a tight, punchy kick, with a poppy snare and wide-open toms. Find out what you like and what feels good, then make it your own. The type and placement of microphones is a big factor in how the drums will sound (for studio as well as live situations). If possible, work with a knowledgeable sound engineer and learn all you can. If that's not an option, do it yourself. Figure out what type of sound you want, and do some research. The internet is an invaluable tool for this. Experiment with different combinations of drums, drum placement, heads, tunings, dampening methods, microphone selections, and mic placement. It's a meticulous and exhaustive process, but achieving a result that you're satisfied with is well worth it.

Technique

The most important aspect of technique is the grip. For matched grip, one widely accepted method is holding the stick between the first knuckle of your index finger and the meat of your thumb (directly on the other side from the thumbnail). This will create what is known as the fulcrum. There should be an imaginary line going through your thumbnail, through the stick, and through the first knuckle of your index finger. The tips of your middle, ring, and pinky fingers then rest on the stick to guide and control it. In general, you play from the wrists with your palms facing down. Although there are a lot of books and videos on this subject, it's wise to seek guidance from a reputable drum instructor to learn the proper mechanics of stick grip.

Once your grip is dialed in, it's time to decide how to use it. In many studio situations, the drummer won't be playing as hard as possible, and may even be playing softer than normal. This facilitates control, fluidity, and cleanly recorded drums. However, nothing is set in stone. Sometimes the drummer may need to play full volume in the studio in order to convey a certain kind of vibe. It depends on what works best for the situation.

The same goes for live playing situations. For example, check out Clyde Stubblefield's playing in some James Brown concert footage. Notice how light he's playing. He's hardly even moving his left wrist, and it's ridiculously funky. However, Clyde has also been quoted in an interview reminiscing about playing a concert at Chicago's Soldier Field. The P.A. system was too small for the venue size so he was "... playing so hard his hands were bleeding." In a lot of live situations, the lighter you play, the funkier it'll be. If you play light, the dynamics of the drums will be better. There will be more texture to the beats. However, there will also be times when you need to hammer out some heavy breakbeats at full volume. Again, it all depends on the situation.

Components of the Drumset

The Snare Drum:

In general, the snare should be the loudest component of the drumset. A good rule of thumb is to play accented snare notes with strokes starting from 8 to 12 inches away from the playing surface. Accented snare notes can also be played as rimshots (playing the center of the drum and the rim simultaneously). This creates a thicker sound which can be used live as well as in the studio. Accented snare notes mainly occur on beats 2 and 4. This is known as the backbeat. These are the beats people clap their hands to. Therefore, the snare plays the most important role in outlining the feel of the beat. In addition, the snare can play unaccented notes. Also known as ghost notes, these are played very lightly near the center of the drum (strokes start from about a half-inch away from the playing surface). They're used to "fill in the cracks," as well as to add flavor and flow to the beat. This should be the softest sound of the drumset. Ghost notes bring the funk to a beat.

You can also play a "rim click" (sometimes called "cross-stick") on the snare. This is achieved by turning the stick around (so you're holding the shoulder and the butt is facing out). Then, you anchor the bottom of your hand (where the wrist and hand meet) in the middle of the drum and use the rest of your hand to lift just the stick (while the bottom of your hand is still anchored). You can then play notes on the rim. You'll get a fuller sound if you play the rim click in line with (i.e., directly above) a tensioning lug.

The Kick Drum:

The kick is tied with the snare as the most important component of the drumset. The kick's main purpose in breakbeat drumming is to play a heavy note on the "one." This establishes the foundation for the beat, which is where the funk originates. Other kick notes help establish the flow of the beat. The kick drum should be the second loudest component of the drumset. For the most part, the volume of the kick is fairly consistent, but mixing it up with accented and unaccented notes will add more flavor to the beat.

The Hi-Hat:

The hi-hat keeps the other components of the drumset together. It helps establish the speed and flow of the beat. It can also be used to communicate volume and aggression. For example, riding on a half-open hi-hat creates a loud, sloshy wash of sound that can add a lot of intensity to a beat. In general, accented hi-hat notes should be slightly softer than the kick drum. They should be played with the shoulder of the stick striking the edge of the top hi-hat cymbal. Unaccented hi-hat notes are equal with ghosted snare notes for the softest sound of the drumset. These are achieved by playing on the top (not the bell) of the hi-hat with the tip of the stick. They're often used to fill in the cracks, and should be blended with the ghosted snare notes. Darker, larger sized hi-hats (14 to 16 inches) tend to work better for breakbeats.

The Toms:

In breakbeat drumming the toms are not necessary. Overusing the toms can distract from the beat. However, they're still used occasionally. When used tastefully, toms can add a sense of drama and increase the energy level of the music. Listen to and analyze the tom sounds of this genre. Experiment to get the sound you want.

The Cymbals:

The cymbals can be used to change the texture of the beat. Riding on a cymbal will make an entirely different beat than if you're riding on the hi-hats. Experiment with getting different sounds out of your cymbals. Playing on the bell (or close to it) will create more of a "ping" sound. Playing closer to the edge will create a wash of sound. You can create different sounds with the cymbal depending on whether you use the tip or the shoulder of the stick. For example, riding on the edge of a big, heavy crash with

the shoulder of the stick will add a lot of power and really open up a breakbeat. Experiment with different hi-hat and cymbal sounds over a constant kick and snare pattern. Crashes are also used to occasionally help punctuate the "one" of the beat, as well as to begin or end a phrase.

Darker, older cymbals (rather than bright, newer ones) tend to be more popular in breakbeats. Again, listen to and interpret the cymbal sounds of different drummers and programmed beats. Experiment and see what you like for your style.

(Note: Some of this information was compiled from the book *Future Sounds* (Alfred Publishing) by David Garibaldi. You should definitely check that one out.)

The Elements:
The Vocabulary of Breakbeat Drumming

Introduction

Breakbeat drumming has its own vocabulary, just as any language does. The breakbeat vocabulary can be divided into thirteen main elements. The manner in which a drummer uses these elements helps to define his/her style. In *The Breakbeat Bible*, the elements are introduced one by one. Each has its own chapter.

After an element is introduced, it is discussed. The discussion includes examples of beats, as well as transcriptions of actual drum breaks that feature the element. Be sure to check out the original songs to get an idea of how the element sounds as part of a recorded drum break. Also listen for how the break fits into the actual song, and how it differs from the drum grooves during other sections of the song. In some cases, an artist that has sampled the break (and for what song) is mentioned. Do some research to find out who else sampled the breaks. Check these other songs out to hear how the breaks were used to make a new song. Don't worry if you can't play the example beats or the transcriptions right away. They're provided to show you what the element sounds like in a beat and looks like on paper. You'll be able to play them after enough practice. (Note: The bpm/time markings (🎵/▶) for the breaks and beats refer to their location in the original recordings. These breaks and beats are not included in *The Breakbeat Bible* audio. See page 178 for a full discussion of the audio.

Each chapter is concluded with a set of exercises and beats that focus on the element being discussed. **To get the full benefit of the exercises and beats, start slowly (60 bpm) and play each example 20 times. Play all of the exercises/beats from the page. Then, gradually increase the tempo and repeat the process.** A good target range for these exercises/beats is between 85 and 105 bpm (the average hip-hop tempo), but you should practice them faster as well. Record yourself practicing these exercises/beats and listen back to make sure your playing is tight. But remember, this is just a suggestion. Any practice at all on these exercises/beats will improve your drumming—but there are no short cuts to playing tight and smooth. If you really want to take it to the next level, you gotta dig deep! Think of these exercises as *Stick Control* for breakbeats. **Approach the exercises and beats of this book with the mindset of a Jedi Knight: focused and patient.**

After the exercises and beats there is an eight-bar phrase relevant to the element covered in the chapter. Get these eight-bar phrases tight at a slower tempo before you increase the bpm. Also, throughout the book there are short biographies of "breakbeat architects." These biographies are devoted so some of the originators as well as some modern-day torch-bearers of breakbeat drumming and hip-hop. Hopefully these biographies will inspire you to check out other architects of the culture.

Before we get into the elements, let's review a few things.

The strongest defining characteristic of breakbeats are their 16th-note subdivisions.

Individual 16th notes are referred to by their name (either "e," "and," or "ah") followed by the number of the beat in which they are appearing (the 1, 2, 3, or 4).

For example, you would refer to the "ah" of one if you wanted to talk about this note:

You would refer to the "e" of three if you wanted to talk about this note:

When referring to a note on any of the downbeats, you just say "on beat 1," "on beat 2," "on beat 3," or "on beat 4."

Swing

When discussing and playing 16th notes, the topic of swing often comes up. 16th notes can be completely straight, as when programmed for certain types of electronic music, or they can be fully swung, like how a jazz drummer plays a ride cymbal pattern or how a blues drummer plays a shuffle. They can also be "in-between-the-cracks" of straight and swung. A lot of New Orleans drummers such as Herlin Riley, Johnny Vidacovich, Zigaboo Modeliste, and Stanton Moore play this way. Some drum machines, such as the Akai MPC, have an option that allows you to apply varying degrees of swing to programmed beats. These are pretty abstract topics that are difficult to translate into words. They're something that you have to hear and feel for yourself. Check out some Three 6 Mafia to hear examples of programmed 16th notes on the hi-hat with no swing. Then check out Art Blakey to hear some really swung shuffles. Check any of the above-mentioned New Orleans drummers to hear some "in-between-the-cracks" playing.

*You can use 16th-note subdivisions to determine the swing of the beat (this only applies to notes on the "e" or the "ah"). Within the context of a 16th-note subdivision, there are two main ways you can play a note.

1 **Playing the note "right down the middle":**

Playing the 16th-note subdivision here creates a straight, tight feeling for the beat. This is common in hip hop and funk beats.

For example, check out this beat:

Track 1

Notice how there's a kick drum note on the "ah" of 1 and snare notes on the "ah" of 2 and the "e" of 3. Play those notes as "down the middle" as you can. Notice how this creates a straight feeling.

2 **Playing the note "behind the beat" or "towards the back":**

Playing the 16th-note subdivision here creates a swung, relaxed, laid-back feeling for the beat. The further towards the back you put it, the more swung it will feel. This is also prevalent in some hip-hop and funk beats.

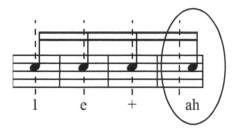

Here's that same beat:

Track 2

This time, play the subdivisions "behind the beat." Notice how this creates that swung, laid-back feel. Experiment with different degrees of "towards the back" placement to create varying degrees of swing.

You can also apply these concepts to the 2 and 4 backbeats, as well as the downbeats.

You can place the backbeats and/or the downbeats slightly (milliseconds) after the underlying pulse of the song occurs. Again, this creates a laid-back feel. This is a very abstract concept that's easier to hear and feel than it is to translate into words. Perhaps the most famous example of "behind the beat drumming" is John Bonham on the Led Zeppelin classic "When the Levee Breaks." Also listen to Al Jackson Jr. from the old Stax records, and Benny Benjamin from some old Motown hits for great examples of playing behind the beat.

Conversely, you can also play ahead of the beat. This means the notes you play occur slightly (milliseconds) before the underlying pulse of the song occurs. This creates an edgier feel. Check out Stewart Copeland of the Police for great examples of playing ahead of the beat.

Take it to the Drums

Here's the drum key for this book:

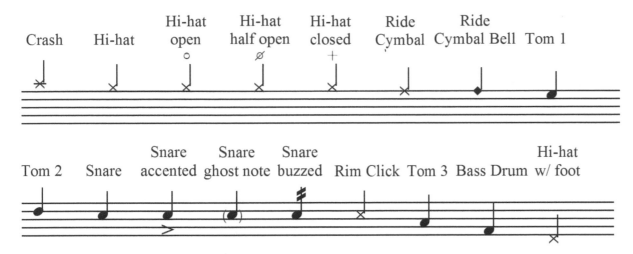

The main drumset components used in the breakbeat style are the kick, snare, and hi-hat.

Here are some of the more common rhythmic patterns you'll encounter in this book, as applied to the the kick, snare, and hi-hat. You'll find these patterns applied to the kick and the snare in different scenarios, but for the purpose of this section they've been depicted on one or the other.

Play the kick and hi-hat together on beat 1, nothing on the "e," the kick and hi-hat together on the "and," nothing on the "ah."

Play the hi-hat on beat 1, nothing on the "e," the hi-hat on the "and," the snare on the "ah."

Play the hi-hat on beat 1, the snare on the "e," the hi-hat on the "and," nothing on the "ah."

Play the hi-hat on beat 1, the kick on the "e," the hi-hat on the "and," the kick on the "ah."

Play the kick and hi-hat together on beat 1, nothing on the "e," the hi-hat on the "and," the kick on the "ah."

Play the hi-hat on beat 1, nothing on the "e," the kick and hi-hat together on the "and," the kick on the "ah."

Play the snare and hi-hat together on beat 1, the snare on the "e," the hi-hat on the "and," nothing on the "ah."

Play the snare and hi-hat together on beat 1, nothing on the "e," the snare and the hi-hat together on the "and," just the snare on the "ah."

Play the hi-hat on beat 1, the snare on the "e," the snare and hi-hat together on the "and," nothing on the "ah."

Play the snare and hi-hat on beat 1, the snare on the "e," the hi-hat on the "and," just the snare on the "ah."

Breakbeats are based on a simple framework consisting of eighth notes on the hi-hat, two and four on the snare, and the kick on beat 1 as well as the "and" of 3.

Here's what that looks like:

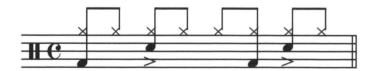

The various elements of the breakbeat style are then added to this framework based on the drummer's stylistic choices, the demands of the musical context, or the raw spontaneity of the moment. (Note: This isn't the only framework beat for the style, but it is one of the most common.)

Other Ideas

1 With a few exceptions, the exercises and beats in this book are written with steady unaccented 8th-note hi-hat patterns. You can also apply the following accented hi-hat patterns to the exercises and beats that contain steady 8th notes on the hi-hat:

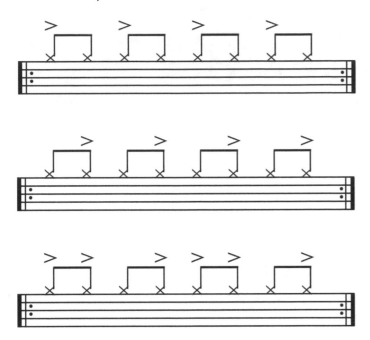

This will change the feel of the exercises and beats, increase your coordination, and help develop the touch and sensitivity of your hi-hat hand.

2 Experiment with different degrees of hi-hat cymbal tightness. For example, applying a lot of pressure to the hi-hat pedal will create a tight hi-hat sound. Conversely, slightly releasing pressure on the pedal will create a looser hi-hat sound. Releasing the pedal further, until the cymbals are slightly separated, creates a loose, sloshy hi-hat sound. Experiment with these concepts as you work through the book.

3 Practice the exercises and beats without the hi-hat part (just kick and snare). This will increase the precision of your kick and snare patterns because you won't have the steady hi-hat part to line them up with. It will also strengthen your internal clock because you won't have the hi-hat keeping steady time.

4 Changing sound sources can dramatically change the beat. Experiment with switching to different sound sources when practicing and playing the exercises and beats of this book. For example, play the hi-hat pattern of a beat on a crash/ride cymbal, or play the snare pattern on a piccolo snare.

5 You don't necessarily have to go through the chapters in order. Practice whatever element you feel you need the most work on, or whatever element you're most interested in adding to your style at the time.

The First Element

The snare playing single 16th-note subdivisions on the "e's" and/or "ah's."

This element adds texture, depth, and dimension to a beat. It also helps determine the swing of a beat, depending on whether you play the subdivisions straight, swung, or in-between-the-cracks. The snare subdivisions on the "e's" and "ah's" are usually ghosted. This means they're played very softly and blended with the hi-hat (refer to the "Components of the Drumset" section on page VIII of the preface). Basically, ghost notes bring the funk to a beat. (Note: The snare subdivisions can also be played mezzo forte (medium loud) or accented. Throughout this book, if a snare note isn't ghosted, or if it doesn't have an accent under it, play it mezzo forte.) **The First Element is a cornerstone of breakbeat drumming.**

Here's what snare notes (ghosted) on the "e" look like:

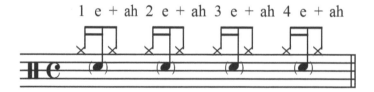

Here's what snare notes (ghosted) on the "ah" look like:

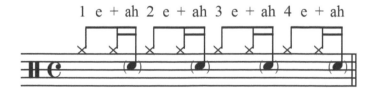

Applying the First Element to Beats

Here's the basic framework beat:

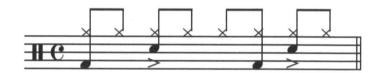

In this example, ghost notes have been added to the basic beat on the "e" of 1, the "ah" of 2, the "e" of 3, and the "ah" of 4:

Track 3

Play through both example beats. Notice how the ghosted snare notes add an extra layer of texture. The second groove has depth. The ghost notes add soul, and bring the basic framework to life. Mastering the First Element will help create a solid foundation for your drumming.

"Unwind Yourself"
Marva Whitney
It's My Thing (King, 1969)

This break features the great **Clyde Stubblefield** on drums. Notice the ghosted snare notes on the "ah" of 2 and the "e" of 3. The break occurs at the intro.

♩ ≈126 bpm
▶ 0:00

The drums (and the opening sax line) from this song were sampled for **The 45 King's "The 900 Number"** from the album ***Master of the Game*** (Tuff City, 1988). Check this one out; it's a classic.

"Youthful Expression"
A Tribe Called Quest
People's Instinctive Travels and the Paths of Rhythm (Jive, 1990)

Notice the ghosted snare notes on the "ah" of 2 and the "ah" of 4. They add just enough texture, which makes the beat really come to life.

♩ ≈109 bpm
▶ 0:17

This song is based on a sample from **Reuben Wilson's "Inner City Blues,"** off the album ***The Sweet Life*** (Groove Merchant, 1974). Notice the enhanced kick drum sound applied to **Thomas Derrick's** original drum pattern.

Single 16th-Note Subdivisions on the Snare: **Exercises**

These exercises will help you play the snare on the "e's" and "ah's." They have basic kick and hi-hat patterns, allowing you to focus on the more intricate snare patterns. In order to develop control and a light touch with the left hand (or right hand for lefty drummers), you should also practice these exercises with the snare notes ghosted and accented.

*You can also benefit from practicing these exercises without the hi-hat pattern. It'll strengthen your kick and snare timing.

Remember to start slow (60 bpm) and gradually increase the tempo.

Single 16th-Note Subdivisions on the Snare: **Beats**

These beats feature single 16th-note subdivisions on the snare. The kick and hi-hat patterns for these beats are basic. This allows you to focus on the more intricate snare patterns.

*You can also benefit from practicing these beats without the hi-hat part. You'll be more solid on them when you bring the hi-hat back in.

Remember to start slow (60 bpm) and gradually increase the tempo.

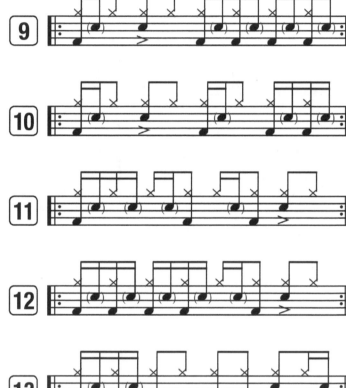

Once you're comfortable with the First Element beats, play the following beat before each of them:

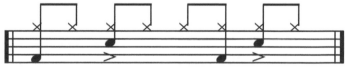

This will make each beat into a two-bar phrase. Repeat each new two-bar phrase 20 times, then move on to the next one.

Single 16th-Note Subdivisions on the Snare: **8-Bar Phrase**

Track 8

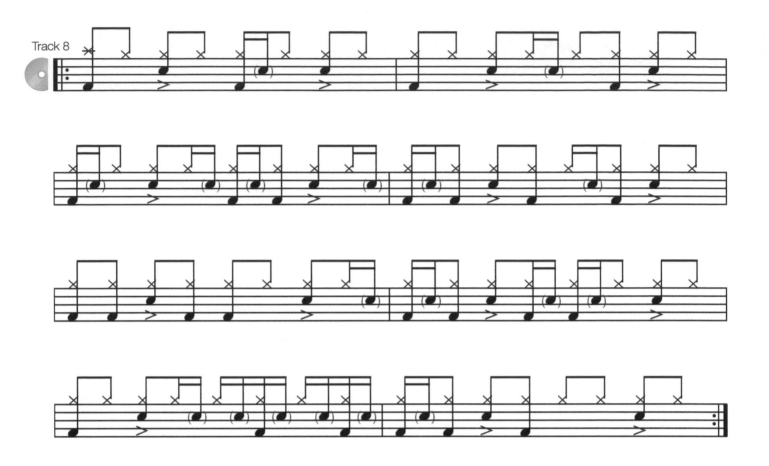

After you're comfortable with the eight-bar phrase, apply it to the following grid:

Groove   8-Bar Phrase

For the initial eight bars of groove, use any beat from this chapter, or make up your own.

clyde stubblefield

Clyde was born on April 18th, 1943 in Chattanooga, Tennessee. He began drumming on tin can lids and cardboard boxes as a child. He went on to play with Otis Redding, and would later achieve notoriety during his tenure with James Brown. Stubblefield joined forces with "The Godfather of Soul" in 1965 as a second-string drummer. Legend has it that Brown witnessed Stubblefield performing in a club, and was blown away by his playing. At the time, Clyde didn't know about James Brown, and was therefore skeptical when invited to audition for his band. He decided to go for it, and the audition took place in a coliseum as people were filing in for the show. Clyde reminisces: "When I first joined James Brown's band, there were five drumsets on stage. I was the sixth. He usually only used three at a time. After I joined, he got rid of three. Jabo and I wanted to play more, so we had to find a way to get rid of that other guy. It finally happened, and Jabo and I ended up being the only two drummers in the band" (*Modern Drummer*, July 2007). Stubblefield's first number-one hit with James Brown was "Cold Sweat," released in the summer of 1967. The B-side to this single was "Cold Sweat (Pt. 2)" which featured a tight drum break. Clyde was beginning to get recognition as a superstar drummer. This was only the beginning. In 1970, James Brown released "Funky Drummer (Pts. 1 & 2)." The song was based on the rock-solid funk foundation of Stubblefield's drumming, and featured a ridiculous eight-bar drum break. The "Funky Drummer" break would go on to become one of the most sampled breakbeats of all time. It's been used on thousands of rock, pop, hip-hop, and electronica recordings by everyone from Run-DMC to Sinead O'Connor. See page 134 of the Breakbeat Transcriptions chapter for more information on the "Funky Drummer" break. Although he hasn't received any royalties from the extensive sampling of his drumming, Clyde Stubblefield has attained legendary status for his contributions to music. He's royalty among musicians and his rep grows bigger. (www.drummerworld.com) (www.answers.com)

The Second Element
The kick drum playing single 16th-note subdivisions on the "e's" and/or "ah's."

This opens up a lot of possibilities for creating variety within a beat. It also helps determine the flow and swing of a beat. The Second Element is very prevalent in breakbeat drumming.

Here's what kick drum notes on the "e" look like:

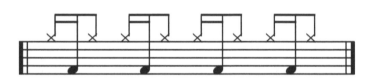

Here's what kick drum notes on the "ah" look like:

Applying the Second Element to Beats

Here's the basic framework beat:

In this beat, kick subdivisions have been added to the basic beat on the "ah" of 1 and the "e" of 2:

Track 9

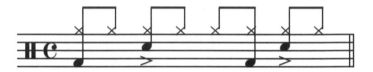

Play through both of the previous examples. Notice how those kick drum subdivisions add variety and flow to the beat. Mastering the Second Element will also help create a solid foundation for your drumming.

*A kick drum note on the "and" of 3, followed by another on the "e" of 4 is a popular pattern in hip-hop beats. This is demonstrated in the following beat.

"Don't Say Nuthin"
The Roots
The Tipping Point (Geffen, 2004)

This beat features the great **Ahmir "Questlove" Thompson** on drums. Notice the kick drum notes on the "and" of 3 as well as the "e" of 4 in the first measure, leading into a kick note on beat 1 of the second measure.

♩ ≈99 bpm

▶ 0:09

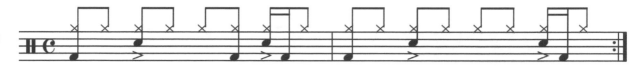

THE ARCHITECTS ::
questlove

Ahmir Khalib Thompson (a.k.a. Questlove) was born on January 20, 1971 in Philadelphia, Pennsylvania. He's best known as the drummer for The Roots. Questlove is a breakbeat drumming master.

His father was a singer in a doo-wop group. A young Thompson often accompanied his father on tour. By age 7, he was playing drums on stage with his father's group. At age 13 he became the musical director. His parents then enrolled him in the Philadelphia High School for the Creative and Performing Arts. There, he formed The Square Roots with rapper Tariq Trotter (a.k.a. Black Thought). They dropped the "Square," and The Roots went on to become international superstars. In 1992, as the band was in its infancy, Ahmir was influenced by groups that sampled breaks from the funk and soul music he grew up on. These progressive groups included A Tribe Called Quest, Gang Starr, and De La Soul. His drumming goal early in his career was to sound like the breaks those guys were using (*Modern Drummer*, March 2005). His early musical studies

focused on jazz, but he wanted to speak the language of hip-hop. He set out to develop a raw style that would be respected by the hip-hop world, as well as serious jazz musicians. His result is a unique drum style that's precise, organic, rooted in funk, and always serves the song. Questlove draws his influence from funk pioneers such as Clyde Stubblefield and Steve Ferrone, while applying it in the manner of a looped breakbeat sample. He exemplifies the full circle of drummers replicating producer's loops of samples of drummers.

Questlove is also an important producer. As a founding member of The Soulquarians production collective, he's responsible for originating the Neo-Soul movement. He's produced critically acclaimed albums for such artists as Common, D'Angelo, Erykah Badu, and Al Green. He also served as the music director for Chappelle's Show. The Roots are currently the house band for the Jimmy Fallon Show, allowing Questlove to bring his breakbeat mastery to the masses on a nightly basis. (www.drummerworld.com)

"School Boy Crush"
Average White Band
Cut the Cake (Atlantic, 1975)

This break features **Steve Ferrone** on drums (Ferrone replaced original drummer Robbie McIntosh, who died of a heroin overdose). Notice the kick drum notes on the "ah" of 2 and the "e" of 3. This is a good example of the Second Element in a classic drum break. The break occurs during the intro.

♩ ≈ 88 bpm
▶ 0:00

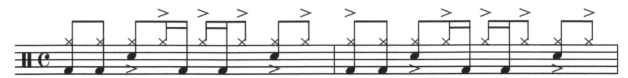

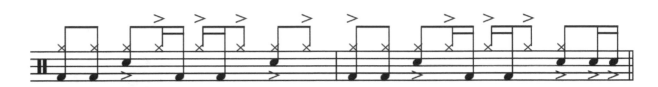

This break was sampled (and slightly sped up) for the **Nas** song **"Halftime,"** from the album ***Illmatic*** (Columbia, 1992). Sometimes producers will only sample part of a break. For "Halftime," Large Professor (the producer of the track) only used the first half of the first measure of the "School Boy Crush" break. He then looped that half measure for the "Halftime" beat.

"Baby This Love I Have"
Minnie Riperton
Adventures in Paradise (Epic, 1975)

This song features **Jim Gordon** on drums. The break starts at the beginning of the song. Notice the kick drum notes on the "e" of 2.

♩ ≈ 82 bpm
▶ 0:00

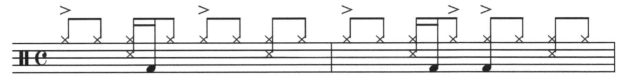

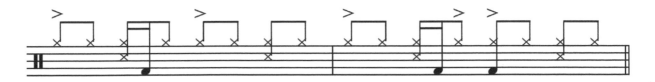

This drum groove, and the accompanying bass line, were sampled and sped up for the song **"Check the Rhime"** by **A Tribe Called Quest** off the album ***The Low End Theory*** (Jive, 1991). For this track, Ali Shaheed Muhammad (the producer of the track) added extra kick drum notes. He also doubled Jim Gordon's original rim clicks with a snare sound. This makes the beat pop a little more.

Also check out **"Play Dis Only at Night"** by **Pete Rock**, on the album ***Petestrumentals*** (BBE, 2001).

Single 16th-Note Subdivisions on the Kick: **Exercises**

These exercises have steady eighth notes on the hi-hat and no snare. This allows you to focus on the more intricate kick drum patterns. Concentrate on the space between the hi-hat notes, and get the kick drum right in there.

This is also a good time to play around with varying degrees of swing. Experiment with placing the kick drum notes closer to the downbeats (the 1, 2, 3, or 4) or the upbeats (the "and's"). Get familiar with how this creates different levels of swing (depending on how close you place the kick note to the hi-hat note). Remember to start slow and record yourself.

Track 10

Track 11

Once you're comfortable with these exercises, add the snare on 2 and 4, or on all of the downbeats (1, 2, 3, 4).

Single 16th-Note Subdivisions on the Kick: **Beats**

These beats have basic snare and hi-hat patterns. This allows you to focus on the more intricate kick drum patterns. It's important to start these slow, and gradually increase the tempo. The beats will feel rushed and uneven if you go too fast too soon.

Once you're comfortable with the Second Element beats, play the following beat before each of them:

This will make each beat into a two-bar phrase. Repeat each new two-bar phrase 20 times, then move on to the next one.

Single 16th-Note Subdivisions on the Kick: **8-Bar Phrase**

Track 14

After you're comfortable with the eight-bar phrase, apply it to the following grid:

Groove   8-Bar Phrase

For the initial eight bars of groove, use any beat from this chapter, or make up your own.

Review Phrases
Elements One and Two

The First and Second Elements often occur in conjunction with each other. The following eight-bar phrases combine the First and Second Elements. The hi-hat plays steady eighth notes. Make sure you keep the hi-hat smooth and even. Don't let the snare rhythms and accents alter the steadiness of the hi-hat pattern. Throughout the rest of the book, you'll find instances of the First and Second Elements in various combinations with each other.

Track 15

After you're comfortable with these phrases, apply them to the following grid:

Groove   8-Bar Phrase

For the initial eight bars of groove, use any beat from the previous two chapters, or make up your own.

The Third Element
The snare playing two 16th notes in a row with one hand.

This can occur on either the "and-ah's," the "e-and's," the "1-e," "2-e," "3-e," or "4-e," or the "ah-1," "ah-2," "ah-3," or "ah-4." The Third Element adds texture, color, and depth to a beat. Also, like the First and Second Elements, it can be used to determine the swing of a beat. With this element, there are different combinations of accents and ghost notes. Sometimes both notes will be ghosted. Sometimes both will be mezzo forte. Occasionally, the first note will be accented and the second ghosted. This is known as a control stroke, and will be discussed later in the chapter. Sometimes the first note will be ghosted, and the second will be accented. This is known as a pull out, and will also be discussed later in the chapter. **The Third Element is a cornerstone of breakbeat drumming.**

For now, let's start simple.

Here's what the snare notated on the "and-ah's" looks like:

Within the context of a full groove, this usually occurs on the "and-ah" of beat 2 and/or the "and-ah" of beat 4.

In this beat, the snare is playing ghost notes on the "and-ah" of 2:

Track 17

Two 16th notes in a row on the "and-ah" are often mixed with single snare subdivisions (the First Element). Check it out:

Track 18

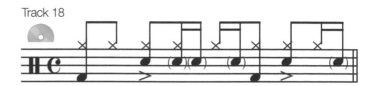

Play through the previous examples. Notice the extra texture, color, and depth created by those ghosted snare notes (especially the instances of "two in a row").

"Take Me to the Mardi Gras"

Bob James

Two (CTI Records, 1975)

This break features the inimitable **Steve Gadd** on drums. Notice instances of the Third Element in the first and third measures. This four-bar break occurs at the intro.

♩ ≈104 bpm

▶ 0:00

This break was sampled for the **Run-DMC** song **"Peter Piper,"** from the album ***Raising Hell*** (Profile, 1986). Rick Rubin and Russell Simmons (the producers of the track) added processed kick, snare, and high-hat patterns. Although it kind of covers up Gadd's original drum pattern, it really fattens up the beat.

Here's what the snare notated on the "e-and's" looks like:

Within the context of a full drum beat, this usually occurs on the "e-and" of beat 1 and/or the "e-and" of beat 3. Remember, nothing is set in stone. It can occur anywhere in the measure.

In this beat, the snare is playing ghost notes on the "e-and" of 3:

Track 19

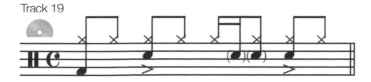

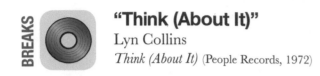

"Think (About It)"
Lyn Collins
Think (About It) (People Records, 1972)

This break is from Lyn Collins' cover of James Brown's "Think (About It)." Lyn's version is backed by the JB's, and features **John "Jabo" Starks** on drums. It was released in 1972 on People Records (a label founded and co-owned by James Brown). Check out other artists from this label as well. This break occurs at 1:21, and again at 2:02 in the song. It contains a good example of the Third Element in a classic drum break. (Note: The open circle over the hi-hat note on beat 1 of the second measure means that it's an open hi-hat note. This topic will be discussed in the Fifth Element chapter.)

≈113 bpm
1:21

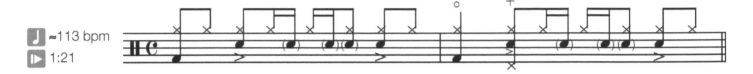

This break has been sampled countless times. For example, it was sampled and slowed down for the **Heavy D and the Boyz** song **"You Ain't Heard Nuttin Yet,"** from the album ***Big Tyme*** (MCA Records, 1989). DJ Eddie F (the producer of the track) slightly chopped up the original break in order to create the new beat. He also enhanced it with a percussion part.

Now we'll get into control strokes and pull outs...

Control Strokes

Control Strokes occur when there are two 16th notes in a row played with one hand. The first note is accented, and the second note is ghosted. This is achieved by playing a full stroke for the accented note, then allowing the tips of your middle, ring, and pinky fingers to control the rebound from that stroke in order to achieve the ghost note. It's one smooth motion, as opposed to two separate motions.

Control strokes usually occur on a downbeat (1, 2, 3, or 4) and the following "e":

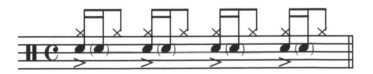

Control strokes most commonly appear with the accented note falling on beat 2 or 4. However, this is not always the case. For instance, there could be an accented note on the "and," followed by a ghost on the "ah."

Here's an example of a beat that contains a control stroke. Notice how the snare plays the accented note on beat 2, then immediately plays a ghost note on the "e" of 2:

Track 20

Control strokes are often mixed with other ghost notes, like this:

Track 21

Play through the previous examples. Notice how the control strokes add another layer of depth to the beats.

"Chinese Chicken"
Duke Williams and the Extremes
Monkey in a Silk Suit is Still a Monkey (Capricorn Records, 1973)

This break features **Earl Young** on drums. Young was a force to be reckoned with on the 1970s Philadelphia funk/soul/R&B studio scene. This is a four-bar break. The first bar contains a control stroke on 2, the second bar contains a control stroke on 4, and the fourth bar contains a control stroke on 2. Look out for other subdivisions on the snare (both ghosted and accented). The break occurs @ 1:40.

♩ ≈116 bpm
▷ @ 1:40

(Note: The hi-hat note with an open circle over it on the "and" of 4 in the second bar is an open hi-hat note. This is discussed in the Fifth Element Chapter. This is an advanced break, so don't worry if you can't quite play it right away. For now just listen to how those **control strokes** sound in the context of a classic drum break.)

Pull Outs

Pull outs also occur when there are two 16th notes in a row played with one hand. However, this time the first note is ghosted, and the second is accented. This is achieved by playing the ghost note as you're lifting your wrist to play the accented note. You play the ghost note as your wrist is pulling up (your wrist is pulling up, but your hand and the stick are moving downward, towards the drum head), then right away you snap your wrist to play the accented note. Again, this is done is one smooth motion, as opposed to two separate motions. This is an advanced concept. Check out the book *It's Your Move* (Alfred Publishing), by Dom Famularo and Joe Bergamini, for a more in-depth discussion of control strokes and pull outs.

Pull outs usually occur on the "ah" followed by the next downbeat.

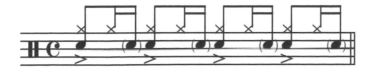

They most commonly occur with a ghost note on the "ah" of 1 followed by an accented snare note on beat 2, or a ghost note on the "ah" of 3 followed by an accented snare note on beat 4. But, again, they can occur anywhere.

Here's an example of a beat that contains a pull out. Notice the ghost note on the "ah" of 3 followed by the accented note on beat 4:

Track 22

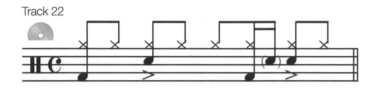

"Squib Cakes"
Tower of Power,
Back to Oakland (Warner Bros., 1974)

This break features the legendary **David Garibaldi** on drums. The first and second bars feature pull outs, and the third bar also contains a pull out (notice the ghost note on the "e" of 3 followed by the accent on the "and" of 3). This break occurs at the beginning of the song.

♩ ≈112 bpm
▶ 0:00

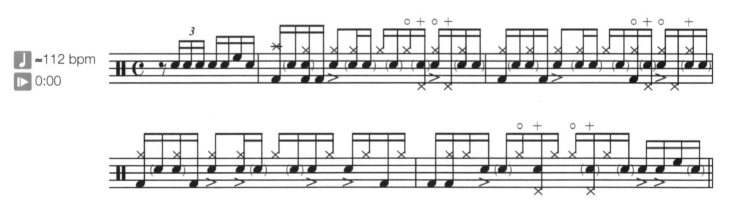

This break contains control strokes in addition to pull outs. It also contains elements we haven't covered yet, such as open hi-hat notes and two 16th notes in a row on the kick drum. This is an advanced break. Don't worry if you can't play it yet. For now just follow along and listen to how the **pull outs** sound in the context of a classic drum break.

You can also play a pull out into a control stroke.

This is achieved by performing the pull out, and then using the accented note of the pull out as the first note of the control stroke. Again, it's all done in one smooth motion, but you're playing three notes. The first note is ghosted, the middle note is accented, and the third note is ghosted. Clyde Stubblefield was one of the first drummers to use this in funk drumming. He's a modern-day master of this technique.

Here's what that looks like within the context of a beat:

Track 23

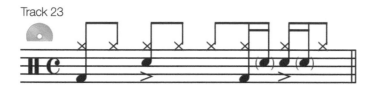

This is an advanced technique which will require a lot of practice to get sounding smooth. Take it slow at first; you may want to begin as slow as 40 bpm. Gradually increase the speed. With enough patience and focus, you'll be able to get this sounding like Clyde. Feel free to move on to the rest of the book before you have this concept mastered. It's something you'll have to constantly work on over a long period of time—not something you learn in a week.

"Ain't It Hard"
Sharon Jones and the Dap Kings
Dap Dippin' With... (Daptone Records, 2002)

This break features the great **Homer Steinweiss** on drums. Make sure you check out some other artists on **Daptone Records** as well. The second bar features a pull out into a control stroke. This four-bar break starts @ 1:32.

≈113 bpm

@ 1:32

"Mother Popcorn (Pts. 1 & 2)"

James Brown

[released as a single (King, 1969)]

Although not an actual drum break, perhaps the most famous example of the pull out into the control stroke features **Clyde Stubblefield** on drums. This song was originally released as a two-part single in 1969 on the **King** record label. If you don't already have this one, make sure you get it off the *Star Time* compilation, which contains the full-length, 6:16 version.

♩ ≈117 bpm

▶ 0:00

This is a difficult beat to play. Take it slow at first, then gradually increase the tempo.

THE ARCHITECTS ::

david garibaldi

David Garibaldi was born on November 4th, 1946 in Oakland, California. He plays drums for the legendary funk band Tower of Power. He began playing drums in the Pleasanton Elementary School band at the age of ten. He got his first pro gig, with the Sid Reis Big Band, when he was a senior in high school. Upon receiving a draft notice for the Vietnam War, he opted to join the Air Force to avoid being sent overseas. This led him to the 724th USAF Band, which was stationed at McChord Air Force Base in Tacoma, Washington. After leaving the Air Force, Garibaldi began playing on the Oakland music scene. Up until this time, he felt the most respectable thing a musician could do with their art was to become a jazz player. However, rock and funk music were gaining popularity and becoming viable occupations for the professional musician. David witnessed a James Brown concert and decided he wanted to be a funk drummer. Developing his own voice became a primary goal. At this point the singer and bass player of the Tower of Power watched David play in a club, and invited him to check out their band. He was impressed, and joined the Tower of Power in 1970 (replacing the singer's brother).

The social upheaval occurring in the San Francisco area during the early 1970s was reflected in Tower of Power's music. All band members participated in the song writing process, and they all wanted to originate as opposed to imitate. After recording their first album, *East Bay Grease* (San Francisco Records, 1970), Garibaldi realized he had a limited vocabulary on the drumset. He didn't want to repeat himself musically, so he began developing different grooves for each song. Eventually, he'd create a different drum groove for each section of a song. This led him to develop a uniquely progressive drum style. Garibaldi created some of the most classic drum breaks of all time, including those found in "Squib Cakes" and "Ebony Jam."

In addition to Tower of Power, Garibaldi has performed/recorded with Boz Scaggs, The BBC Orchestra, The Buddy Rich Orchestra, and Talking Drums. He's also an important educator, and author of classic texts such as *Future Sounds* (Alfred Publishing) and *The Code of Funk* (Hudson Music). (www.towerofpower.com) (www.drummerworld.com)

Two 16th Notes in a Row on the Snare: **Exercises**

These exercises will help you play the different versions of the Third Element. The exercises are grouped into five different categories. They all contain steady eighth notes on the hi-hat and steady quarter notes on the kick. This will allow you to focus on the more intricate snare patterns. Again, feel free to experiment with applying swing to these exercises.

These categories are not necessarily meant to be practiced in a sequential order. For example, if you feel you need extra practice with pull outs, spend more time on the pull out section. You can revisit these exercises as you proceed through the rest of the book, or even after you've finished it. **You can also benefit from practicing these exercises without the hi-hat patterns.** Remember to start slow and gradually increase the tempo.

Two 16th notes in a row: **both are mezzo forte**

Track 24

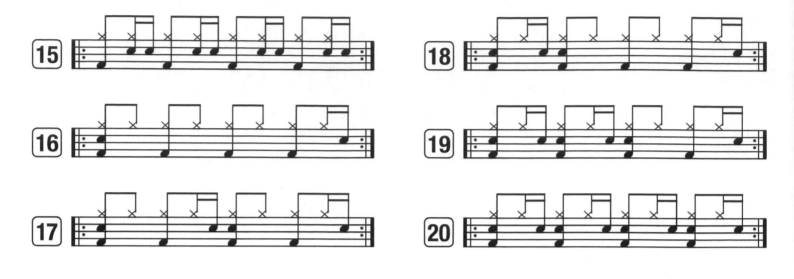

Two 16th notes in a row: **both are ghosted**

Track 25

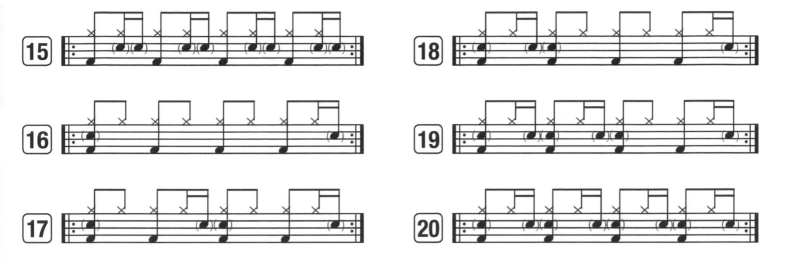

Two 16th notes in a row: **control strokes**

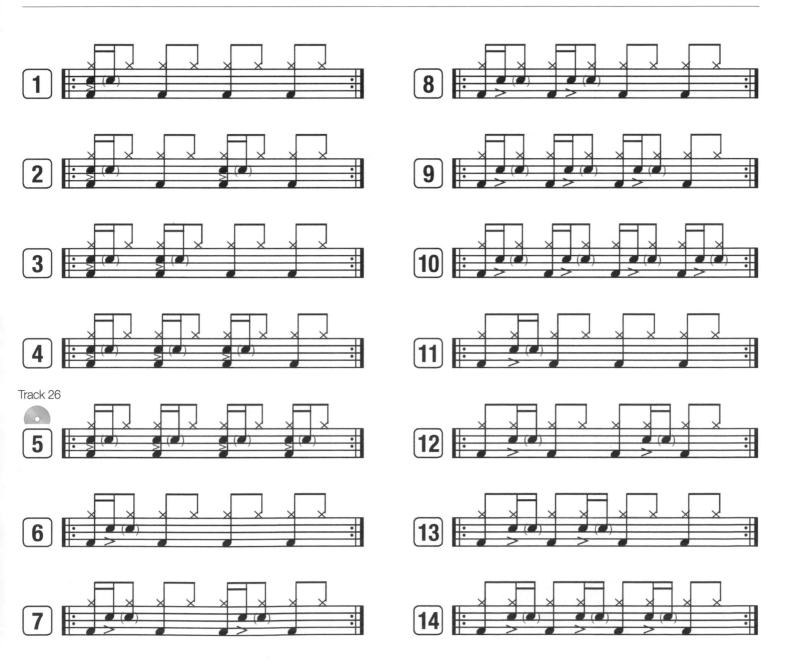

Track 26

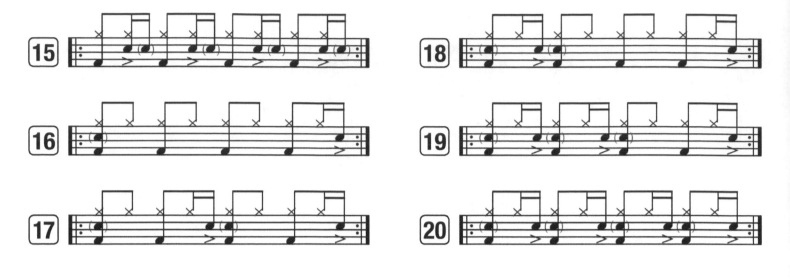

Two 16th notes in a row: **pull outs**

Track 27

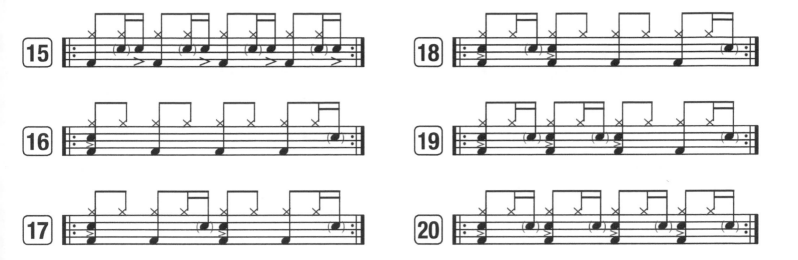

Two 16th notes in a row: **mixed patterns**

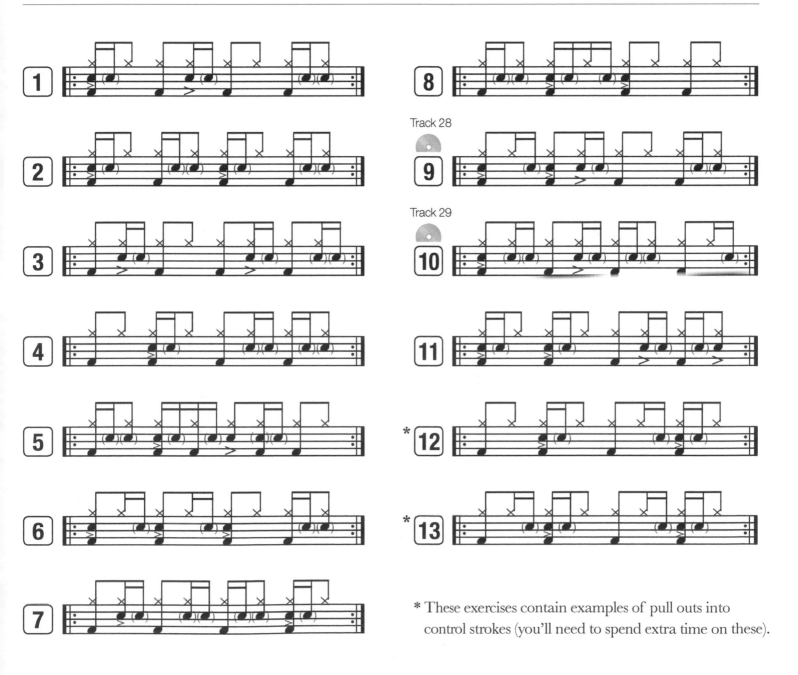

Track 28

Track 29

* These exercises contain examples of pull outs into
control strokes (you'll need to spend extra time on these).

Two 16th Notes in a Row on the Snare: **Beats**

These beats have simple kick and hi-hat patterns so you can focus on the snare patterns. In addition to the two 16th notes in a row on the snare, the beats also contain some single 16th-note subdivisions on the snare (the First Element). Again, do your best to keep the hi-hat smooth (don't accent it when the snare is accenting). Feel free to apply swing to these beats. However, keep in mind that breakbeats are usually straight or "in-between-the-cracks" of straight and swung.

Start slow (60bpm) and gradually increase the tempo. Again, you may want to practice these beats without the hi-hat pattern. This will help strengthen your kick and snare timing.

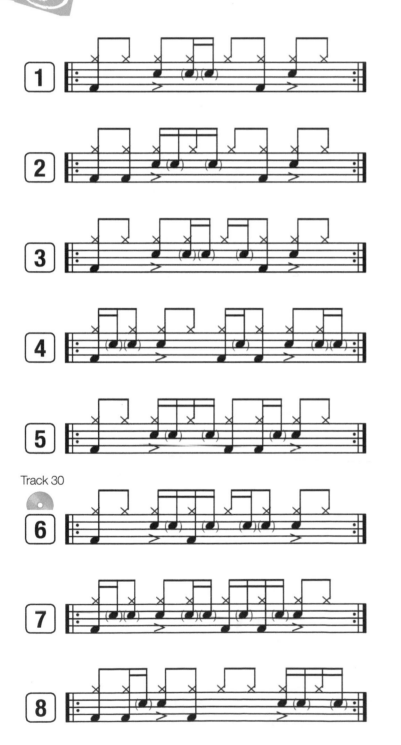

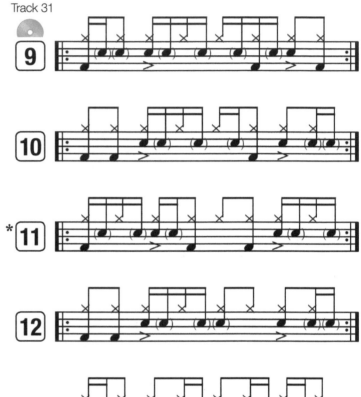

Once you're comfortable with the Third Element beats, play the following beat before each of them:

This will make each beat into a two-bar phrase. Repeat each new two-bar phrase 20 times, then move on to the next one.

* These beats contain examples of pull outs into control strokes. Spend some extra time with these to get a good flow going.

Two 16th Notes in a Row on the Snare: **8-Bar Phrase**

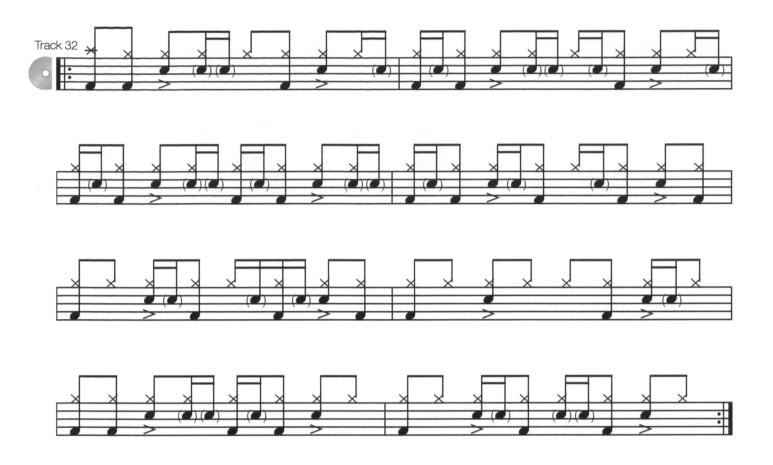

Track 32

After you're comfortable with the eight-bar phrase, apply it to the following grid:

Groove   8-Bar Phrase

For the initial eight bars of groove, use any beat from this chapter, or make up your own.

The Fourth Element

The kick drum playing two 16th notes in a row.

This adds a lot more power and strength to a beat. It also opens a new realm of possibilities for creating variety within the groove. Like the first three elements, it also helps determine the flow and swing. The Fourth Element is another cornerstone of breakbeat drumming. **Remember, regardless of what is happening in the rest of the measure, the kick usually plays a slightly accented note on beat 1.**

Here's what the kick drum notated on the "1-e," "2-e," "3-e," and "4-e" looks like:

Here's the basic framework beat:

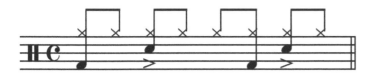

Here's the basic beat with a kick note added on the "e" of 1. Now there are two 16th notes in a row:

Track 33

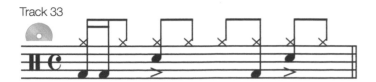

Play through the previous example beats. Notice the difference. Placing that extra kick note on the "e" of 1 adds a lot more drive to the beat. There's a little more going on, and the groove is more interesting. You don't need to add much to create a big impact. Keep this in mind as your skill level increases and you work through the rest of the book. More often than not, the simpler your beats are, the better they'll sound and feel.

This concept can also be mixed with single kick drum subdivisions (the Second Element), which leads us to...

"Films"
Gary Numan
The Pleasure Principle (Atco, 1979)

This break, featuring **Cedrick Sharpley** on drums, illustrates the Fourth Element. The break occurs @ 0:05.

♩ ≈99 bpm
▶ 0:05

This song was sampled for the **GZA** song **"Life is a Movie,"** from the album **Pro Tools** (Babygrande Records, 2008). GZA, who also produced the track, basically just used a few different measures from "Films" as is for the "Life is a Movie" beat. It sounds tight, and that fill at the end of the second measure of the "Films" break loops throughout "Life is a Movie."

Here's what the kick drum notated on the "e-ands" looks like:

Once again, here's the basic beat:

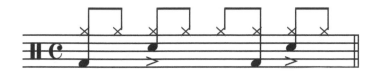

Here's the basic beat with a kick note added on the "e" of 3. You now have two 16th notes in a row on the kick:

Track 34

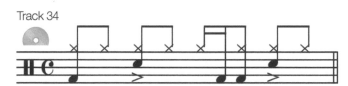

Play through the previous examples and notice the difference. Adding that kick note on the "e" of 3 adds bounce to the beat. This will have a big effect on the sound and feel of the groove.

This concept can also be mixed with single kick drum subdivisions, which leads us to...

"Funky President (People It's Bad)"
James Brown
Reality (Polydor, 1974)

The break occurs at the intro of the song. Notice the kick drum on the "e-and" of 3 in each measure. Check this one out, it's a classic.

(Note: The open circle over the hi-hat note on the "and" of 3 means that it's an open hi-hat note. This topic is discussed in the next chapter. Also, the snare note with two slashes on the "ah" of 4 in the second bar is a buzz stroke. This topic is discussed in the Seventh Element chapter.) There are two versions of this song. One version is 99 bpm, and the other is 105 bpm.

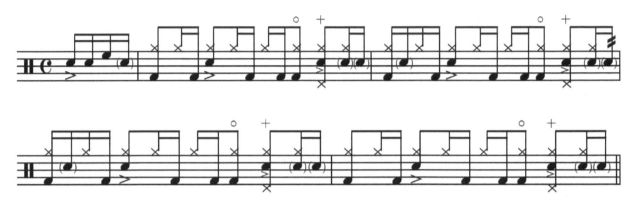

This break was sampled for **Slick Rick's "Why, Why, Why"** from ***The Art of Storytelling*** (Def Jam, 1999). Slick Rick, who also produced the track, used the first measure of the "Funky President" break as is for "Why, Why, Why." He also added a bass part.

The kick drum notated on the "and-ahs":

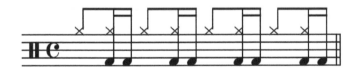

Here's a basic beat:

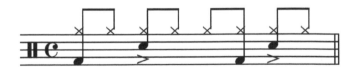

Here's the basic beat with kick notes added on the "and-ah" of 1:

Track 35

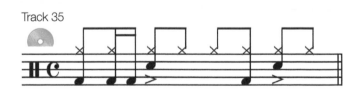

Play through the example beats. Notice how the extra kick notes add forward momentum and help shape the beat. They also add some variety.

"It's a New Day"
The Skull Snaps
Skull Snaps (GSF, 1973)

This break, featuring **George Bragg** on drums, illustrates the kick playing on the "and-ah" of 3. The break occurs at the intro of the song.

♩ ≈95 bpm

▶ 0:00

This is another break that's been sampled countless times. It was used for **The Pharcyde** classic **"Passin Me By"** from ***Bizzare Ride II The Pharcyde*** (Delicious Vinyl, 1992). J-Swift (the producer of the track) chopped up the "New Day" break, and mixed those drum sounds with processed drum sounds in order to create the "Passin Me By" beat.

Here's the kick drum notated on the "ah-1," "ah-2," "ah-3," and "ah-4":

The basic beat:

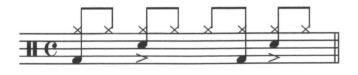

Here's the basic beat with a kick note added on the "ah" of 4. Now there are two 16th notes in a row on the kick:

Track 36

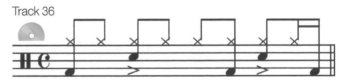

Play through both of the previous example beats. Notice how that kick note on the "ah" of 4 helps to push the beat back around to the 1. A kick drum note on the "ah" of 4 followed by another on the downbeat creates more bounce. It's a good way to increase the "head-nod" factor, which leads us to...

"Get Out of My Life, Woman"
Lee Dorsey
The New Lee Dorsey (Stateside, 1966)

This break occurs at the intro of the song. Check out the grainy, lo-fi drum sound. This track possibly features Joseph "Zigaboo" Modeliste on drums.

This break has been used countless times. It was sampled (perhaps most famously) and slowed down for the **Biz Markie** song **"Just a Friend,"** from the album *The Biz Never Sleeps* (Cold Chillin', 1989). It was also used for the **Big Daddy Kane** song **"Brother, Brother"** from the album *Prince of Darkness* (Cold Chillin', 1991). Big Daddy Kane, who also produced the track, paired the "Get Out of My Life" break with a few other samples to create one of the sickest hip-hop beats of all time.

The kick drum on the "ah-1" concept is very prevalent in the programmed drum patterns of hip-hop.

"Above The Clouds"
Gang Starr
Moment of Truth (Noo Trybe Records, 1998)

Notice the swing of the kick drum pattern, as programmed by the great DJ Premier:

Final Notes

In general, if the second of two kick drum notes in a row lands on an "e" or "ah," it will add forward momentum. If it falls on a downbeat (1, 2, 3, or 4) or an upbeat (the "ands"), it will create more bounce. You're going to need some extra kick drum chops to pull off the Fourth Element, so make sure you spend some extra time on this chapter's exercises.

THE ARCHITECTS :: dj premier

Chris Edward Martin (a.k.a. DJ Premier) was born on March 21, 1966 in Houston, Texas. His childhood was split between Houston and Brooklyn. By the time he studied computer science at Prairie View A & M outside of Houston, Premier had learned various instruments and managed a record store. Moving back to Brooklyn in 1987, he joined forces with the late, great Guru to form the legendary duo Gang Starr. The group specialized in blending hip-hop with jazz, and their beats were very sample-heavy. This project helped to shape Premier's production style. DJ Premier represents another step in the chain of evolution from the original breakbeat drummers to the modern-day hip-hop culture. He's one of the most important producers of the 1990s. In addition to Gang Starr, he has collaborated with

Nas, The Notorius B.I.G., Jay-Z, Jeru the Damaga, Mos Def, Big Daddy Kane, and Branford Marsalis, among many others. His beat production style is distinctive and raw. It's characterized by sparse loops and heavy drums. One of his trademarks is scratching short vocal samples from multiple artists in order to create a chorus. He's known for sampling from jazz, funk, and soul. He'll also sample from an artist's past work when making a new track for them. Premier is heavily influenced by New York hip-hop innovators such as Marley Marl, Jam Master Jay, and Afrika Bambaataa. *The Source* magazine named Premier one of the top five hip-hop producers of all time, and About.com ranked him the number one hip-hop producer of all time. (www.allmusic.com)

These exercises have steady eighth notes on the hi-hat, and no snare. This will allow you to focus on the kick drum patterns. These exercises may seem simple and basic, but don't just gloss over them and move on. Use them to really focus on the quality of your kick drum performance at various tempos. Focus on the performance of high-quality, consistent kick drum notes, placed exactly where you want them. This way, your accuracy and sound quality will increase (this is especially helpful for studio sessions). Remember to start slow (60 bpm) and gradually increase the tempo. As you get comfortable with these, you can add 2-and-4 backbeats or steady quarter notes on the snare.

Two 16th Notes in a Row on the Kick: **Beats**

These beats contain basic snare and hi-hat patterns, allowing you to focus on the more intricate kick drum patterns. It's important to start these slow and gradually increase the tempo. This will give you good flow and control for the kick drum notes. If you play too fast too soon, the beats will be rushed and uneven. Again, feel free to experiment with the swing factor, but remember that most breakbeats are usually straight or "in-between-the-cracks." Don't forget to record yourself practicing these beats.

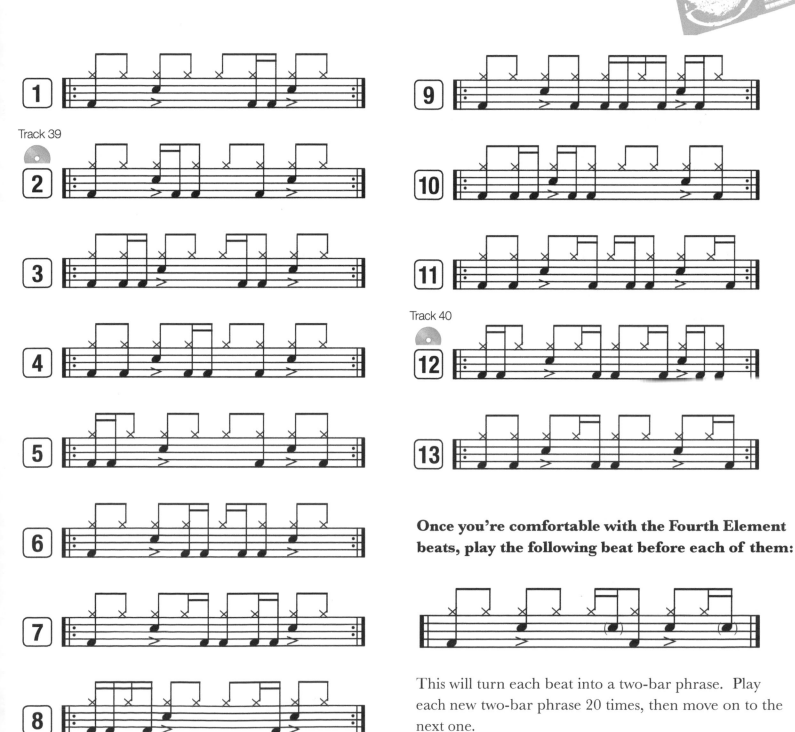

Track 39

Track 40

Once you're comfortable with the Fourth Element beats, play the following beat before each of them:

This will turn each beat into a two-bar phrase. Play each new two-bar phrase 20 times, then move on to the next one.

Two 16th Notes in a Row on the Kick: **8-Bar Phrase**

Track 41

After you're comfortable with the eight-bar phrase, apply it to the following grid:

Groove   8-Bar Phrase

For the initial eight bars of groove, use any beat from this chapter, or make up your own.

Review Phrases:
Elements One, Two, Three, and Four

The first four elements often occur in conjunction with each other, in various combinations. The following eight-bar phrases combine the first four elements. The hi-hat plays eighth notes. Keep the hi-hat steady as you practice/play through these phrases. Throughout the rest of the book, you'll find instances of the first four elements mixed together in various combinations.

Track 42

1

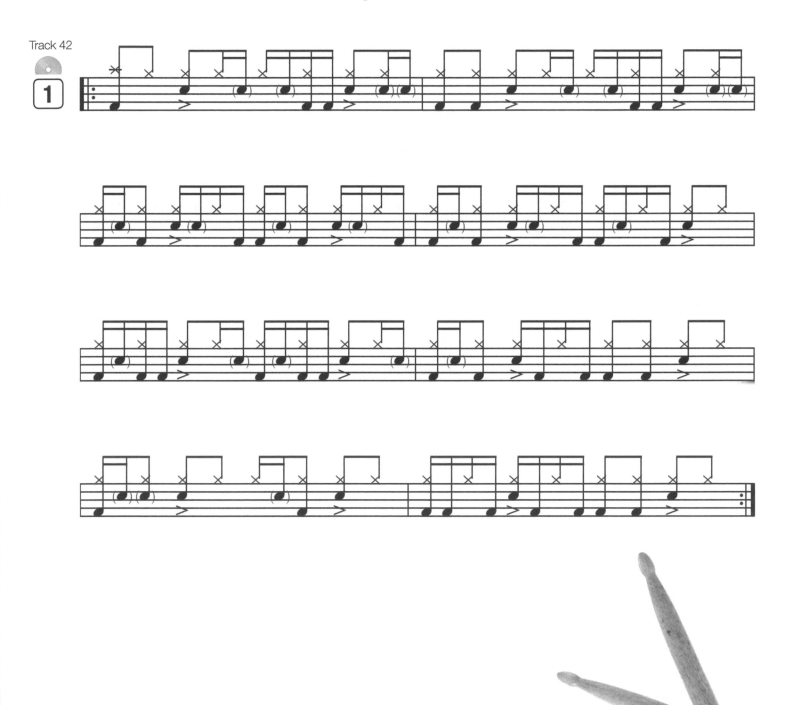

Track 43

After you're comfortable with the eight-bar phrases, apply them to the following grid:

For the initial eight bars of groove, use any beat from the previous four chapters, or make up your own.

Bonus Exercise:

These exercises feature the four different paradiddle inversions played between the kick and snare. Practicing these will give you a great power workout covering the first four elements. Playing these without the hi-hat pattern will improve your kick and snare timing. Remember to start slow and gradually increase the tempo.

First, let's review the four paradiddle inversions.

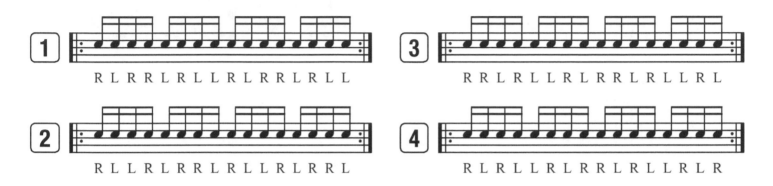

1 R L R R L R L L R L R R L R L L

3 R R L R L L R L R R L R L L R L

2 R L L R L R R L R L L R L R R L

4 R L R L L R L R R L R L L R L R

Here are the exercises:

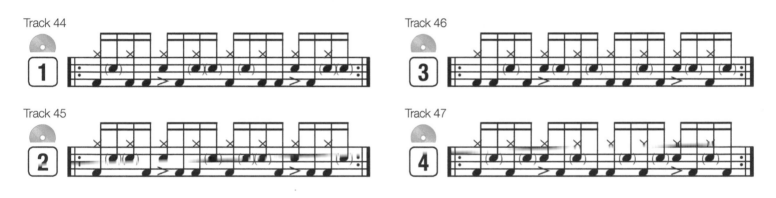

Track 44 — **1**

Track 45 — **2**

Track 46 — **3**

Track 47 — **4**

The Fifth Element
An open hi-hat note.

This adds flavor to a beat, but requires extra coordination. It's formed by opening the hi-hat with the left foot and playing it with the right hand, then closing it with the left foot (when you close the hi-hat with your foot, you can also play it at the same time with your stick, but you don't have to). The open hi-hat is notated with an open circle over the hi-hat note. This element occurs frequently in breakbeat drumming. However, you don't want to overuse the Fifth Element, or your grooves will sound more like disco beats than breakbeats.

There are two main versions (and a third, less common version) of open hi-hat notes.

1. **The first version** is opening the hi-hat for the value of one eighth note. This can occur on any beat of the measure, but is typically found on the "and" of 1 or the "and" of 3.

This beat features an open hi-hat note on the "and" of 3. The open note ends with the closing of the hi-hats with the left foot on beat 4:

Track 48

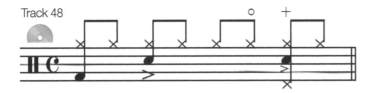

This beat features an open hi-hat note on beat 3. The note ends with the closing of the hi-hats with the left foot on the "and" of 3:

Track 49

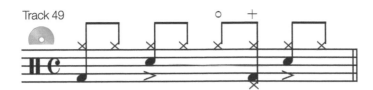

"I Want'a Do Something Freaky to You"

Leon Haywood

Come and Get Yourself Some (20th Century, 1975)

Notice the open hi-hat on the "and" of 3 in the second and fourth bars. The break is at the intro of the song.

♩ ≈94 bpm

▶ 0:00

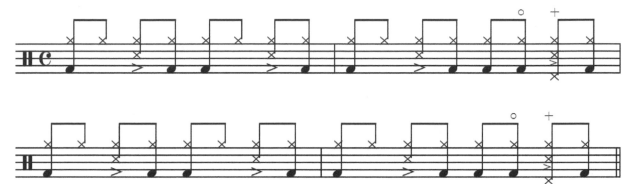

This break was most famously sampled for **"Nuthin' but a G Thang"** by **Dr. Dre featuring Snoop Dogg**, from the album ***The Chronic*** (Death Row, 1992). Check out the enhanced kick drum sound from Dre's beat. He also used a few other samples from "I Want'a Do Something Freaky to You" for "Nuthin' but a G Thang."

"Impeach the President"

The Honeydrippers

(Alaga Records, 1973)

Check the open hi-hat on the "and" of 3 as well as the stellar drum sounds. The break occurs at the beginning of the song. (Note: Notice the two 16th notes leading directly into an 8th note on the hi-hat. Play this with one hand. This concept is discussed in the Ninth Element chapter. Also, check out the slight swing of this beat.)

♩ ≈97 bpm

▶ 0:00

This is another break that's been sampled countless times. It was used for the **Nas** youth empowerment anthem, **"I Can,"** from his album ***God's Son*** (Columbia, 2003). Salaam Remi (the producer of the track) used the first measure of the "Impeach the President" break, as is, for the "I Can" beat.

2 **The second version** is opening the hi-hat for the value of one 16th note. This most commonly occurs by opening the hi-hat with the foot and playing it on the "e," then immediately closing it with the foot on the "and." Or, opening the hi-hat with the foot and playing it on the "ah," then immediately closing it with the foot on the next downbeat. It can be found anywhere, though. Wherever this version is played, the hi-hat is closed on the 16th note immediately following the open note.

Here's a one-bar beat that incorporates the second version:

(Note: In order to make the open hi-hat note occur on the "ah" of two, the hi-hat has to play two 16th notes leading directly into an 8th note. With hip-hop style breakbeats, this is often performed with one hand, as opposed to using alternating sticking. These concepts will be further discussed in the Ninth Element chapter. For now, take it slow and focus on making the open hi-hat note sound and feel as good as possible.)

The second version is sometimes linked together in a series of two or more open hi-hat notes. When this happens, the snare can play ghost notes in between the open hi-hat notes. If this occurs, the snare lines up with the closed hi-hat note (left hand and left foot play at the same time). This type of figure is sometimes found at the end of a two- or four-bar phrase...

Here's a four-bar phrase. The first three bars contain the basic beat. The fourth bar features open hi-hat notes on the "e" of 2, the "ah" of 2, the "e" of 3, the "ah" of 3, and the "e" of 4:

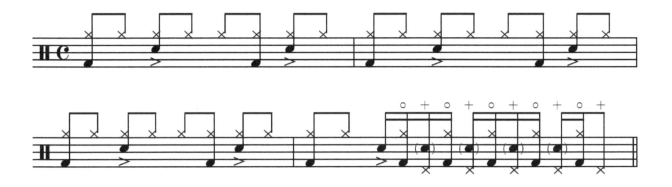

It can also be incorporated into a beat. **Here's another one-bar beat.** This features two open hi-hat notes (of the second version).

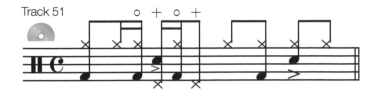

(Note: In order to make the open hi-hat note occur on the "ah" of 1, the hi-hat plays two 16th notes in a row (use one hand). Again, this will be discussed in more detail in the Ninth Element chapter. For now, take it slow and focus on making the open hi-hat notes sound and feel good.)

"Rocksteady"
Aretha Franklin
Young, Gifted, and Black (Atlantic, 1972)

This break features the great **Bernard Purdie** on drums. Notice how he uses the open hi-hat on the "e" of 3, the "ah" of 3, and the "e" of 4 to end his break and bring the rest of the band back in.

≈105 bpm

2:29

The drum/bass/guitar groove at the intro of "Rocksteady" was sampled for **EPMD's "I'm Housin',"** from the album **Strictly Business** (Fresh, 1988).

3 **The third (less common) version:** You'll sometimes find an open hi-hat note on beat 1, with the foot closing the note on beat 2. The open hi-hat note lasts for the full value of a quarter note. This kind of open hi-hat note can also be found on any beat of the measure.

Here's a beat with the third type of open hi-hat note:

Track 52

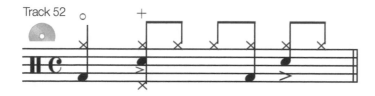

You can also apply the third type of open hi-hat note to a two-bar beat—which will avoid the possibility of the open hi-hat sound occuring too frequently.

Track 53

The three versions of open hi-hat notes can be applied to the same beat, using various combinations.

For example, you could play something like this:

Again, you don't want to overuse this concept.

The manner in which you choose to apply the different versions of the Fifth Element will help define your drumming style.

THE ARCHITECTS ::

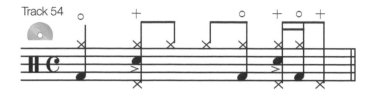

Adam Deitch is a drummer and producer. He's most well known for his work in hip-hop and funk. Deitch first picked up a pair of sticks at the age of two. His great uncle was a drummer, and both of his parents are funk drummers. His first gig was at a school assembly for his kindergarten class. By the age of eight he was sitting in with his parent's respective bands and playing jazz, funk, and R&B. In 1992/1993 he was the house drummer for the Nuyorica Poets Cafe, where he played behind emerging hip-hop superstars such as Mos Def and Erykah Badu. In 1994 he began attending the Berkley College of Music in Boston. There, he became a founding member of Lettuce, a force to be reckoned with for the past fifteen years. Deitch then joined the legendary Average White Band. He stayed with A.W.B. for two years of tours and the recording of a live album. Next, Deitch joined forces with John Scofield for the recording of two albums and multiple tours. Deitch has also performed/recorded with The Game, DJ Quick,

John Medeski, The GZA, DJ Logic, and Rocco Prestia. He currently performs with The Adam Deitch Project and Break Science, among many others. These projects blend hip-hop, Broken Beat, Drum'n'Bass, and dub, and feature acoustic drums and other live instruments mixed with DJs. Deitch is one of the most important players on the scene today, taking the art of breakbeat drumming to the next level.

As a producer, Deitch was first influenced by such artists as Public Enemy and Eric B & Rakim. He began producing by making loops on a tape deck in his bedroom. He's currently a member of various production teams including The Fyre Dept., The Formula, and Gilla Nut House. As a producer he's worked with artists such as 50 Cent, Talib Kweli, Redman, Justin Timberlake, Snoop Dogg, and Immortal Technique. He aims to bring live drums back to pop and hip-hop music. (www.drummerworld.com) (www.royalfamilyrecords.com)

Open Hi-Hat Notes: **Exercises**

These exercises will help you get comfortable with open hi-hat notes. Use them to help refine the sounds you're getting out of the hi-hat. Don't just skim over them; working with just the hi-hat (no kick or snare) will allow you to focus on the quality of sounds you're generating. Experiment with different degrees of tightness/looseness between the hi-hat cymbals (this is achieved with varying degrees of pressure applied to the foot pedal). Make sure everything is even, smooth, and feeling good. With enough practice these will become part of your style. Don't forget to record yourself and analyze the playback. Count out loud when you practice these exercises, and be conscious of whether the stick also plays the hi-hat on the "foot-closing" notes.

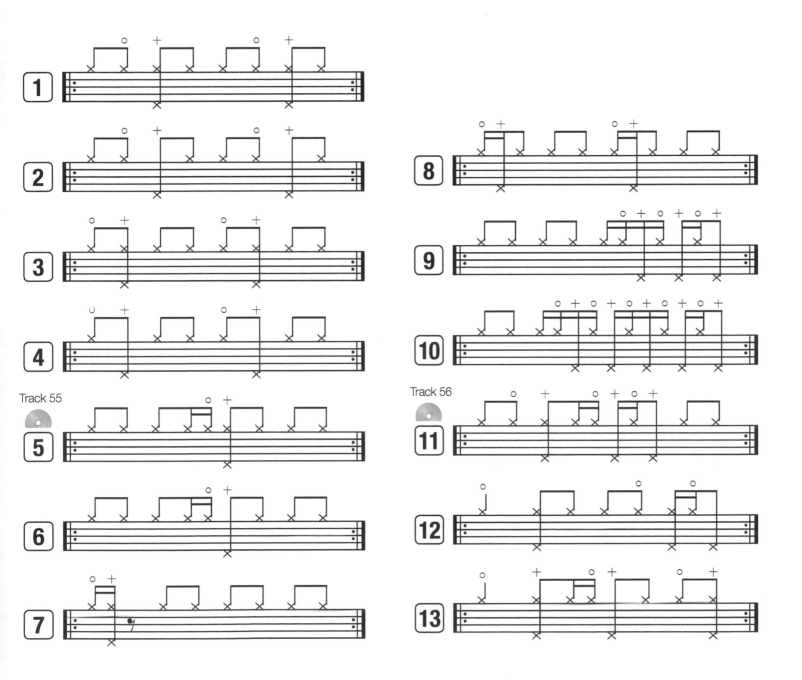

Open Hi-Hat Notes: **Beats**

This section begins with basic kick and snare patterns. This will help you get comfortable with the open hi-hat notes. The beats then gradually increase in complexity as the first four elements are added. Be aware if the stick also plays the hi-hat on the "foot-closing" notes.

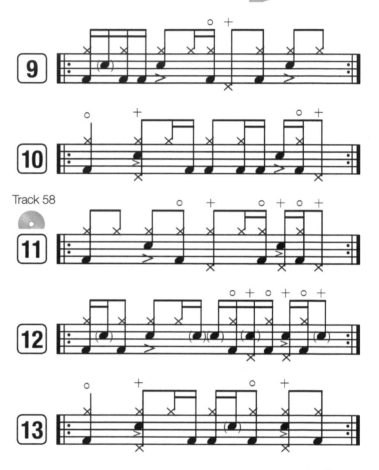

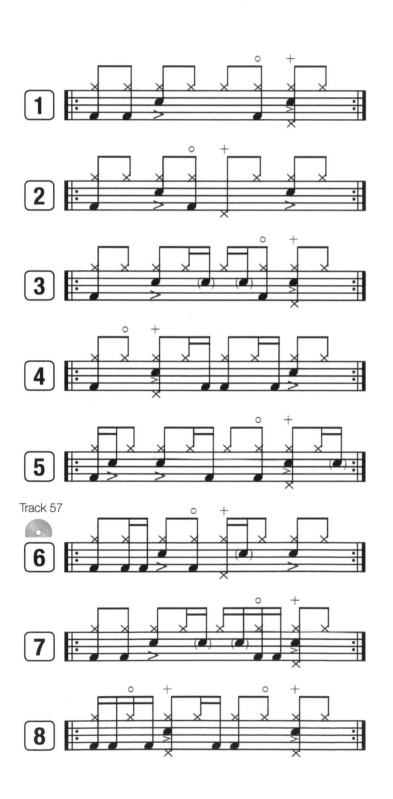

Once you're comfortable with the Fifth Element beats, play the following beat before each of them:

This will turn each of the beats into a two-bar phrase. Play each new two-bar phrase 20 times, then move on to the next one.

Open Hi-Hat Notes: **8-Bar Phrase**

Track 59

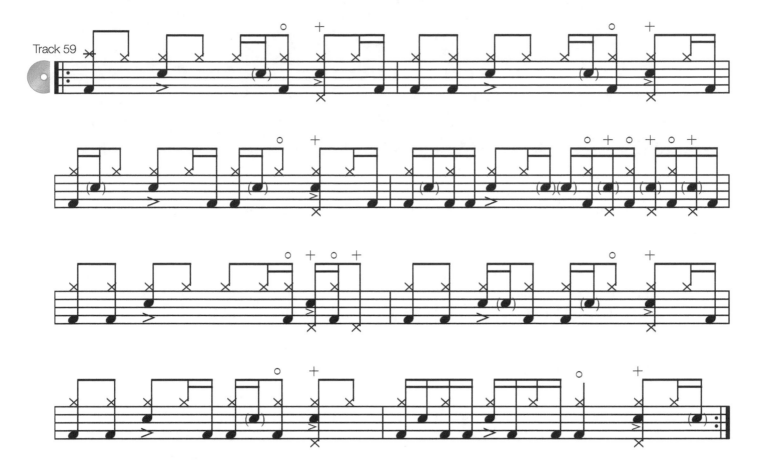

When you're comfortable with the eight-bar phrase, apply it to the following grid:

Groove   8-Bar Phrase

For the initial eight bars of groove, use any beat from the chapter, or make up your own.

The Sixth Element
Syncopated accents on the snare.

This means that you shift the snare accents to places other than beats 2 and 4. This is a very powerful element. The Sixth Element is highly effective for changing up the feel and flow of a beat. It's a good way to add variety without being too flashy. Most beats usually have accented snare notes on the 2 and 4. According to the great Bob Moses, in his book *Drum Wisdom* (Modern Drummer Publications, Inc.), this is "...where the swing resides...These are the beats that you snap your fingers on or clap your hands to." (*Drum Wisdom*, pg. 12) Accenting on these beats creates a very powerful groove. This is why the majority of beats have the snare on the 2 and 4.

When snare accents are syncopated, they are most commonly shifted to the "and" of the beat. Bob Moses speaks more about this in his book: The "and" of 1 and the "and" of 3 "...feel like an elbow in the ribs. They have kind of a jerky feeling that wakes you up. They also remind me of a contraction; they have a 'pulling in' kind of motion. They are very effective because they tend to propel the music." (*Drum Wisdom*, pg. 12) When discussing the "and" of 2 and the "and" of 4, Moses says, "...they are like an expansion rather than a contraction. They are a stretching—a leaning forward." (*Drum Wisdom*, pg. 12) **Based on this information, there are four main ways the Sixth Element can be used to alter the feel and flow of a beat.**

1. **The First**

Here's a beat with steady "2 and 4" snare accents:

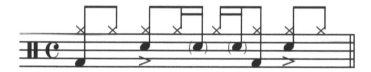

Now here's a beat with an accented snare note on the "and" of 1, and another on beat 4:

Track 60

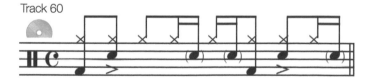

Play through both of the previous example beats. Notice how this type of syncopation creates a jerky, contracting kind of feel.

2 **The Second**

Again, here's a beat with steady "2 and 4" snare accents:

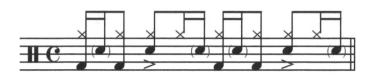

Now here's a beat with an accented snare note on beat 2, and another accented snare note on the "and" of 3:

Track 61

Play through both of the previous example beats. Notice how this type of syncopation also creates that contracting, jabby feeling.

BEATS **"Lost Ones"**
Lauryn Hill
The Miseducation of Lauryn Hill (Columbia, 1998)

This programmed beat features accented snare notes on beat 2, as well as the "and" of 3.

♩ ≈95 bpm
▶ 0:00

These are only the first two measures of the song. The beat for the rest of the song continues in this manner, with slight variations. Notice how the hi-hat isn't playing steady eighth notes—it's playing a broken pattern. This concept is further discussed in the Ninth Element chapter. For now, just focus on how the snare pattern sounds and feels.

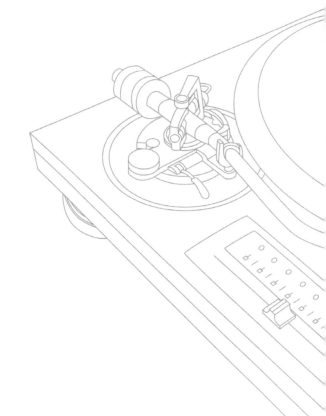

3 The Third

Again, here's a beat with steady "2 and 4" accents on the snare:

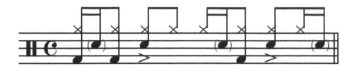

Now here's a beat with the snare playing an accent on the "and" of 2, and another accent on beat 4:

Track 62

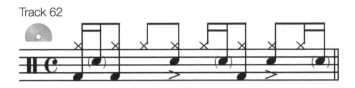

Notice the expanding, "leaning forward" kind of feel that's created by this type of syncopation.

4 The Fourth

Steady "2 and 4" accents on the snare:

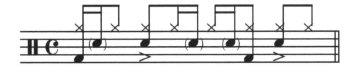

This beat has the snare playing an accent on beat 2, and another accent on the "and" of 4:

Track 63

Again, notice the drawn out, "stretching" feeling this syncopation creates for the beat.

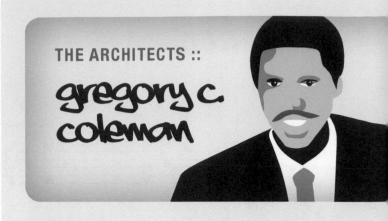

THE ARCHITECTS ::

gregory c. coleman

G.C. Coleman is most well known as the drummer for The Winstons. He played on the infamous "Amen" break, from the song "Amen, Brother." Coleman was born in 1944 and took an interest in drums as a child. He went on to become the drum major for Armstrong High School in Richmond, VA. He also led his own band, G.C. Coleman and the Soul Twisters. A sharp dresser known for his laughter and love of dancing, he went on to play drums with musical giants such as The Marvelettes of Motown, Otis Redding, and Curtis Mayfield. After these experiences, he moved to Washington, D.C. and joined the legendary band The Winstons. With this band he would create musical history, and in the process spawn several subcultures and musical genres. In 1969, The Winstons released a single entitled "Color Him Father." The B-side to this single was "Amen, Brother." The "Color Him Father" single went platinum and received a gold record award from the R.I.A.A. in July of 1969. However, the B-side was destined for infamy. Coleman played a four-bar break in "Amen, Brother." As the late 1970s and early 1980s gave birth to DJing and sampling, artists discovered the "Amen" break. A former employee of Downstairs Records, Breakbeat Lenny, included the "Amen" break in his famous compilation series *The Ultimate Breaks and Beats* in 1986. The popularity of the "Amen" break skyrocketed, and it's now arguably the most popular break of all time. It's been sampled thousands of times for hip-hop, pop, Drum'n'Bass, and Jungle songs. However, G.C. Coleman remains an unsung hero. Neither he nor Richard L. Spencer (copyright owner of the song) received any royalties for the extensive sampling. However, there is a myth that G.C. once received an anonymous gift of $1000 for playing that break. Coleman died in Atlanta in 2006. See page 135 of the Breakbeat Transcriptions chapter for more information on the "Amen" break. (www.ukhh.com) (http://en.wikipedia.org)

"Cold Sweat (Pt. 1)"
James Brown
released as a single (King, 1967)

This song introduced syncopation to pop music. It was first released as a two-part single in 1967. Here's the main drum groove from the song, as played by the master, **Clyde Stubblefiel** :

"Cold Sweat" also marked the first time James Brown requested a drum solo: "...give the drummer some?," which leads us to...

"Cold Sweat (Pt. 2)"
James Brown
released as a single (King, 1967)

The break occurs at 4:27 (you have to get the full-length version of this song in order to hear the break). Perhaps the most easily accessible album that contains the full version is **Star Time** (the version from **20 All Time Greatest Hits** ends at 2:51, and thus doesn't have the break). You can also get the full version as a single on iTunes. The first bar has a syncopated snare note on the "and" of 4. Also, notice the ghost note on beat 4 of the third bar, followed by an accent on the "and" of 4. (Note: The two slashes on the snare note mean that it's a buzz stroke. This topic will be discussed in the next chapter.) This break also has some nice rack tom work.

"75 Bars (Black's Reconstruction)"
The Roots
Rising Down (Def Jam, 2008)

This break features the legendary **Ahmir "Questlove" Thompson** on drums. It's comprised of two different beats. Let's do a comparison.

The break starts right at the beginning of the song. Here's the first beat Questlove plays:

Notice the accented snare notes on beats 2 and 4.

Now, here's the next beat he plays:

Notice how the snare plays on beat 2 (not quite ghosted, not quite accented), but then plays an accented note on the "and" of 2. This is similar to Clyde Stubblefield's beat in the third bar of the "Cold Sweat" break.

Listen to the whole break so you can hear and feel the difference between the two beats. This will help you hear the impact that shifting the accented snare note from beat 2 to the "and" of 2 can have.

The accented snare note can also shift to another downbeat. For example, there could be an accented snare note on beat 2, and another accented snare note on beat 3. When this occurs it is often as part of a two-bar phrase. This is not quite as common, but it's very effective to use occasionally.

Here's a two-bar phrase. The first bar has accented snare notes on beats 2 and 3.

Track 64

"UMI Says"
Mos Def
Black on Both Sides (Rawkus, 1999)

This is one of the tightest beats of all time. You'll find this kind of beat all over different boogaloo and funk songs. Definitely check this Mos Def song though. The beat is a four-bar phrase. The first and third bars have accented snare notes on beat 2 and beat 3, as well as the "and" of 4. The second and fourth bars have accented snare notes on beats 2 and 4. Ghost notes on the snare switch things up and define the four-bar phrase.

The accented snare notes can also be shifted to any of the "e's" or "ah's" in the measure.

This will have the same effects as placing the accents on the "and's," only magnified. In general, placing an accent on the "e" of any beat will create that jerky, contracting feeling. Placing an accent on the "ah" of any beat will create that expanding, stretching feeling. However, this isn't too prevalent in the breakbeat style. You don't want to overuse this either; it can make things a little too choppy. Occasionally use this concept to create diversity in your beats.

This beat has an accented snare note on the "ah" of 1, and another accented snare note on beat 4:

Track 65

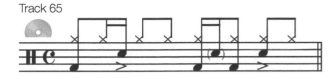

Notice the expanding, stretching feeling this creates.

This beat has an accented snare note on the "e" of 2, and another accented snare note on beat 4:

Track 66

Notice the contracting feeling this creates.

Using the "e's" or "ah's" further expands the possibilities of places to which you can shift the accented snare notes.

Final Notes

Basically, you can shift the accented snare notes anywhere in the measure. It depends on how you want to alter the feel of the beat, or what the music calls for. It's important to listen to a lot of music and check out how shifting the accents on the snare alters the feel of the beat. Use this to make decisions on how you want to apply this element to your own style. With enough listening and practice, syncopated snare accents will flow effortlessly into your playing.

e6 Syncopated Accents on the Snare: **Beats**

Remember to start these slow (60 bpm) and gradually increase the tempo. Make sure you keep everything in the pocket, despite the syncopated snare accents. Don't forget to record yourself and analyze the playback.

Once you're comfortable with the Sixth Element beats, play the following beat before each of them:

This will make each beat into a two-bar phrase. Repeat each new two-bar phrase 20 times, then move on to the next one.

*This is already a two-bar phrase, so don't apply the beat to it.

Syncopated Accents on the Snare: **8-Bar Phrase**

When you're comfortable with the eight-bar phrase, apply it to the following grid:

For the initial eight bars of groove, use any beat from the chapter, or make up your own.

The Seventh Element
Applying buzz strokes and rolls to your beats.

This element adds style, color, and texture to a beat. These strokes are achieved by allowing the stick to bounce one or more times. This is achieved by applying varying degrees of pressure to the stick via your grip. If you've never been in a drum line, or you haven't been keeping up on your practice pad sessions, you might have to experiment a little to get this down. You may also want to search out a reputable drum teacher to help you get this technique dialed in. The buzz strokes on the snare can be placed anywhere in the measure. They can be accented, ghosted, or mezzo forte.

Buzz strokes are notated like this:

♪ **If there's one slash, it means to let the stick rebound twice (you get exactly two notes from one stroke).**

This is typically only used for buzz strokes applied to shorter notes (usually sixteenth notes), and for rolls. It's also known as a double stroke.

♪ **If there are two slashes, it means to let the stick rebound several times (lasting for the length of the note).**

If the buzz stroke is applied to a longer note (such as a quarter note), there will be more rebounds. If it's applied to a short note (such as an eighth or sixteenth note), there will be less rebounds. Again, you'll have to experiment with varying degrees of pressure and release in your grip in order to make this happen. If you want more rebounds (for a longer note), you'll loosen up your grip. If you want less rebounds (for a shorter note), you'll tighten up your grip. Again, you just have to experiment and find what works best for you.

(Note: This is just general notation for the purpose of *The Breakbeat Bible*. You'll find different notations in different books, especially more technical snare drum studies.)

Here's some examples of beats with buzz strokes:

This beat has a buzz stroke on the "ah" of 4:

Track 70

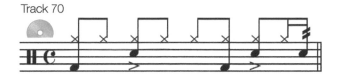

This beat has a buzz stroke on the "and" of 2:

Track 71

Make sure you allow the buzz stroke to last the full value of that eighth note on the "and" of 2.

This beat has a buzz stroke on the "e" of 3:

Track 72

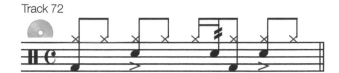

Buzz strokes sometimes occur on accented backbeats. Here's a beat with a buzz stroke on beat 4:

Track 73

Make sure you allow the buzz stroke to last the full value of that quarter note on beat 4. Again, you may need to experiment with varying degrees of pressure and release regarding your grip.

Play through the previous four example beats. Notice the extra layers of color and texture these buzz strokes add to the beats.

BREAKS

"Chocolate Buttermilk"
Kool and the Gang
Kool and the Gang (De-lite Records, 1969)

This song features the great **George Brown** on drums. The break starts at 1:24. Notice the buzz strokes, including the one on the rack tom.

Beats sometimes contain five-stroke rolls. This beat features a five-stroke roll on the snare starting on the "and" of 2. The right hand plays a double stroke on the "and" of 2, the left hand plays a double stroke on the "ah" of 2, and the roll is finished off with the right hand on the hi-hat on beat three:

Track 74

RR LL

"50 Ways to Leave Your Lover"
Paul Simon
Still Crazy After All These Years (Columbia, 1975)

This break features the incredible **Steve Gadd** on drums. It features a five-stroke roll between the snare and kick starting on the "and" of 4 in the second bar, and ending on the 1 as the beat loops. It also features a double stroke on beat 4 of the first bar.

♩ ≈102 bpm

▶ 0:00

This break was replayed (by **Karriem Riggins**) for the **Common** song **"Forever Begins,"** from the album ***Finding Forever*** (Geffen, 2007).

THE ARCHITECTS ::
grandmaster flash

Joseph Saddler (a.k.a. Grand Master Flash) is one of the founding fathers of hip-hop. He's a strong link between the early breakbeat drummers and the modern-day hip-hop culture. Flash was born on January 1, 1958 in Bridgetown, Barbados. His family then emigrated to the South Bronx. By the early 1970s he was studying electrical engineering, which would lead to his concept of using the turntable as an instrument. He began to DJ at block parties. Flash, in addition to Kool Herc, invented the technique of using the same record on two different turntables in order to mix back and forth between the same break. Some say he was the first to actually manipulate records with his hands. Grandmaster Flash began to mark up his records with crayons, fluorescent pens, and grease pencils to help guide his DJ sets. He invented techniques such as the double-back, the back door,

the back spin, and phasing. These helped the DJ create music on the spot by counting and controlling the revolutions of the record. He basically created the foundation for everything a hip-hop DJ does. Some say Flash was the first DJ to invite MCs to rap over his beats. In late 1978 he formed the legendary group Grandmaster Flash and the Furious Five. The group achieved widespread fame with their hit "The Message." In 2007 they were the first rap group to be inducted into the Rock'n'Roll Hall of Fame. Grandmaster Flash has also received the VH1 Hip-Hop Honors Award, the B.E.T. Icon Award, the Bill Gates Vanguard Award, and a Lifetime Achievement Award from the R.I.A.A. He's still releasing albums and has also put out a book entitled *The Adventures of Grandmaster Flash: My Life, My Beats*. (www.grandmasterflash.com)

Buzz Strokes/Rolls: **Exercises**

These exercises will help you incorporate buzz strokes and rolls into your beats. Use these exercises to focus on performing high-quality buzz strokes. Make sure they're clean and well defined. Remember to start slow and gradually increase the tempo. Don't forget to record yourself practicing these exercises.

With the exception of exercise 11, these are written with two slash marks (multiple bounces/buzzes). You can also practice them as if they have one slash mark (double strokes).

Buzz Strokes/Rolls: Beats

These beats will allow you to focus on performing high-quality buzz strokes and rolls. Again, don't forget to record yourself and analyze the playback. Start slowly and gradually increase the tempo.

Once you're comfortable with the Seventh Element beats, play the following beat before each of them:

This will make each beat into a two-bar phrase. Play each new two-bar phrase 20 times, then move on to the next one

Buzz Strokes/Rolls: **8-Bar Phrase**

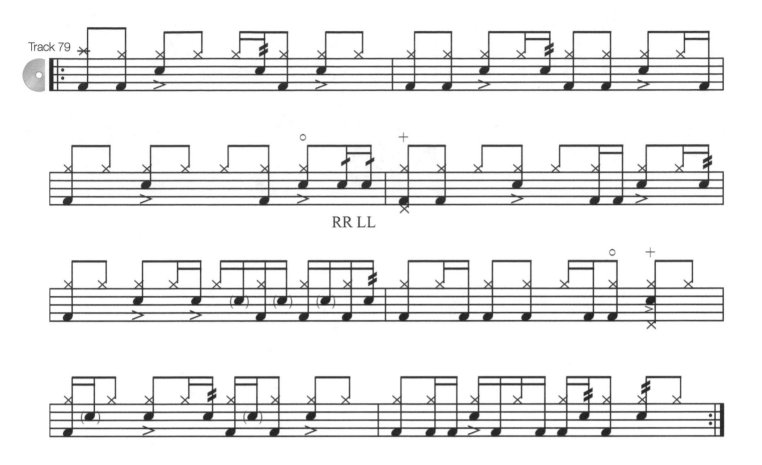

Track 79

RR LL

When you're comfortable with the eight bar phrase, apply it to the following grid.

Groove   8-Bar Phrase

For the initial eight bars of groove, use any beat from the chapter, or make up your own.

e8

The Eighth Element
Steady 16th notes on the hi-hat, played with one hand.

One of the more powerful elements, the Eighth Element creates a solid layer under which to lay the kick and snare patterns. It's easy to lock the kick and snare into a pocket when you line them up with a steady 16th note hi-hat pattern. This element provides the listener with a very consistent rhythm to lock in with, drawing listeners and dancers into a trance-like, altered mind state. Since the hi-hat is playing on every 16th note, this element can be used to determine the swing of a beat. It also allows for more effortless maintenance of steady time. In addition, playing all of the hi-hat notes with one hand (as opposed to alternating) allows your other hand to focus on the snare patterns (without having to break up the flow of the hi-hat). This element is often performed with a light touch, using the tip of the stick. It usually occurs at tempos of 105 bpm or slower. You can often hear the Eighth Element in the programmed drum patterns of contemporary genres such as hip-hop, Trip-Hop, Downtempo, and Dubstep.

Here's the basic framework beat:

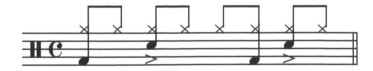

Now here's the same kick and snare pattern with steady 16th notes on the hi-hat:

Track 80

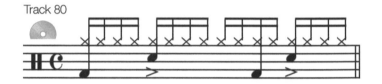

Play through both of the previous example beats. When you bring in the Eighth Element, notice how the beat tightens up; it's easier to lock in that kick/snare pattern. The downside to this element is that unless you've spent years working on the Moeller technique (or other speed development studies), you'll only be able to use this element for slower tempos. That's okay, because we often need the most help locking in and holding steady during slower tempos. You can keep the toes of your hi-hat foot pressed on the pedal while tapping out quarter notes (or eighths) with your heel. This will also help you keep solid time.

Various kick/snare patterns (from the first four elements), as well as other elements (such as open hi-hats, syncopated snare accents, and buzz strokes/rolls), can be played under the steady 16th-note hi-hat pattern of the Eighth Element. When, where, why, and how they're applied is based on the stylistic choices of the drummer, the demands of the music, or both.

This example features a control stroke:

Track 81

This example features buzz strokes:

Track 82

This example features a syncopated snare accent:

Track 83

This example features an open hi-hat note:

Track 84

This is a good time to experiment with varying degrees of tightness/looseness on the hi-hat cymbals (very tight, medium, or loose). Test them out on the previous examples, as well as the exercises and beats of this chapter.

You can also accent the hi-hats on the downbeats along with lighter notes on the "e-and-ah." This works well with a half-open hi-hat, and is useful for heavier playing situations. Check it out:

Track 85

BREAKS

"Breakthrough"
Isaac Hayes
Truck Turner (Stax, 1974)

The break occurs at the beginning of the song. It features steady 16th notes on the hi-hat and a nasty kick/snare pattern.

♩ ≈84 bpm

▶ 0:00

This break was sampled, slightly sped up, and chopped up for **Jay-Z's "Empire State of Mind,"** off his 2009 release **The Blueprint 3** (Roc Nation). It sounds as if Shux, the producer of the track, used most of the first measure of the "Breakthrough" break. He then chopped and slightly rearranged it to create the "Empire State of Mind" beat.

"SpottieOttieDopaliscious"
Outkast
Aquemini (LaFace Records, 1998)

This beat features the steady 16th-note hi-hat pattern of the Eighth Element over a tight kick/rim click pattern, as played by **Victor Alexander**. Notice the 32nd-note rim click at the end of the second measure. This creates an implied triplet feel, which helps gives the beat that floaty feeling. (Note: After 1:10, Alexander plays the hi-hat on the "ah" of 4 in the second bar).

♩ ≈63 bpm
▶ 0:06

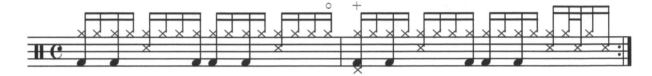

Recap

The Eighth Element can help you lock in, tighten up, and keep a steadier tempo during slower grooves. It can also draw listeners and dancers into a trance-like, altered mind state. However, your hi-hat hand will eventually get tired. It's difficult to maintain steady 16th notes with one hand on the hi-hat at faster tempos. Therefore, this element is mostly used in conjunction with tempos of 105 bpm or slower. Regardless, there's something special about the feel created by playing the 16th notes with one hand. Perform the Eighth Element as your chops will allow (but don't stress and strain too much). Practicing one-handed 16th notes on a pillow will help you build up your chops for this element. You can also study the Moeller technique. This is another matter entirely, and there are a lot of good books, videos, and teachers out there that can help you with this.

(Note: Perhaps the most famous drum break featuring the Eighth Element is the "Funky Drummer" break. This is discussed on page 134 of the Breakbeat Transcriptions section.)

Steady 16th Notes on the Hi-Hat with One Hand: **Exercises**

These exercises will help you line up different kick and snare patterns while playing steady 16th notes on the hi-hat. No snare accents or ghosts have been written in. Practice these with the snare notes mezzo forte (medium loud); also as accents and ghost notes. Remember to start slow. Maintain an even feel on the hi-hat. Don't strain your hi-hat hand attempting to play too fast too soon. Gradually build up the tempo, and you'll develop a more relaxed hi-hat hand. Use these exercises to experiment with varying degrees of swing. When doing this, start with the 16th notes completely straight, then gradually morph to being completely swung (Stanton Moore's book and DVD series, *Groove Alchemy* (Hudson Music), has excellent sections on playing straight, swung, and in-between-the-cracks). Also experiment with applying different amounts of pressure to the hi-hat foot pedal (to create different degrees of tightness/looseness between the two hi-hat cymbals).

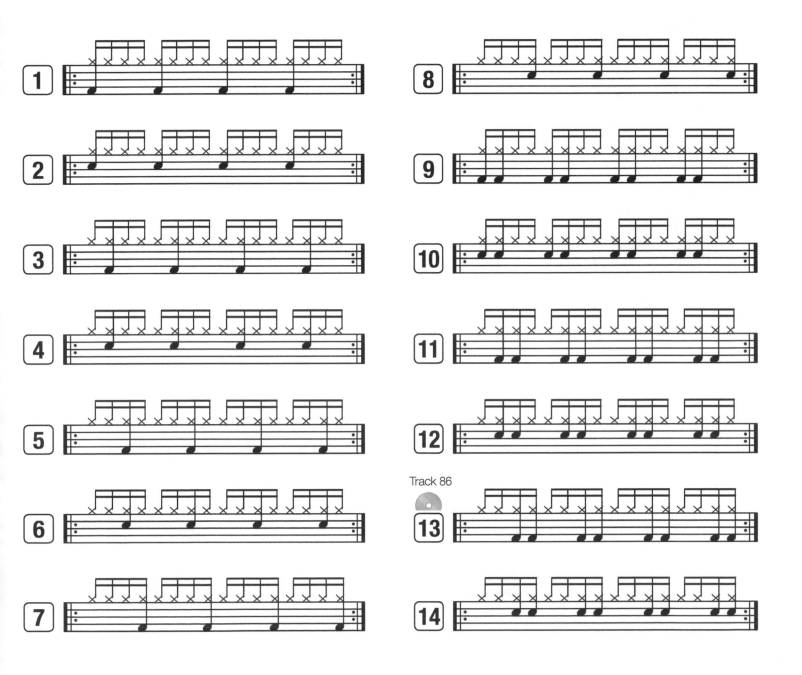

Track 86

Track 87

THE ARCHITECTS ::
stanton moore

Stanton was born and raised in New Orleans, Louisiana. While growing up he absorbed the rich musical heritage of his city. Second Line brass bands played an extremely influential role in his development as a drummer. Stanton also apprenticed with New Orleans drum legend Johnny Vidacovich. While attaining a Bachelor's degree in music and business from Loyola College, Moore co-founded Galactic in the early 1990s. Tight grooves and heavy touring led to widespread success for the band. Stanton currently collaborates with a long list of contemporary artists, in projects such as Garage A Trois, Dragon Smoke, and most recently, Street Sweeper Social Club (with Tom Morello and Boots Riley). In addition to this, Moore has released four solo albums: 1998's *All Kooked Out*, 2001's *Flyin' the Koop*, 2006's *III*, and 2008's *Emphasis! (On Parenthesis)*. Stanton is also an active teacher and clinician, spreading his knowledge of New Orleans music around the world. He's the author of the book/DVD series *Take It To The Street* (Carl Fischer), and has recently released a DVD/book series entitled *Groove Alchemy* (Hudson Music), covering his approach to funk drumming. The book and DVD are a companion to the Stanton Moore Trio's 2010 release, *Groove Alchemy*. Not only is Stanton Moore carrying the torch for New Orleans drumming, he's a breakbeat master taking the art of drumset playing to the next level. (www.drummerworld.com) (www.stantonmoore.com)

Steady 16th Notes on the Hi-Hat with One Hand: **Beats**

These beats have steady 16th notes on the hi-hat and various kick and snare patterns. When practicing these, make sure you can maintain a steady volume on the hi-hat pattern. Also, look out for instances of the other elements added to some of these beats. Experiment with applying different amounts of swing. Also, experiment with varying degrees of hi-hat cymbal tightness/looseness.

Track 88

Track 89

Once you're comfortable with the Eighth Element beats, play the following beat before each of them:

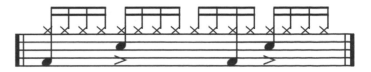

This will make each beat into a two-bar phrase. Repeat each new two-bar phrase 20 times, then move on to the next one.

Steady 16th Notes on the Hi-Hat with One Hand: **8-Bar Phrase**

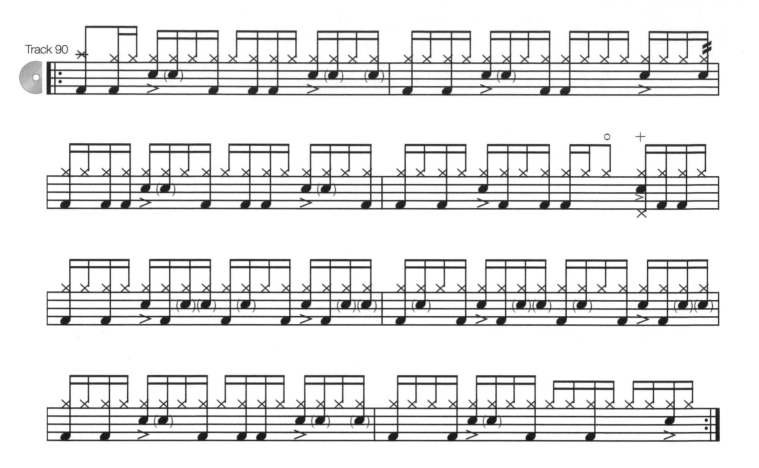

When you're comfortable with the eight-bar phrase, apply it to the following grid:

Groove   8-Bar Phrase

For the initial eight bars of groove, use any beat from the chapter, or make up your own.

The Ninth Element

Mixing up the hi-hat pattern with different combinations of 8th notes, 16th notes, and rests.

Depending on how it's utilized, this element can really push a beat forward. It can also break up the flow of a beat when rests are used. You can mix this element with ghosted snare notes to create a steady stream of 16th notes. In addition, the Ninth Element can be performed with alternating sticking. Alternating sticking will help you play "in-between-the cracks" of straight and swung. It's also useful for creating a steady stream of 16th notes at higher tempos. This is the complete opposite end of the spectrum from the Eighth Element. However, the Ninth is another useful tool for being able to fully serve the music. This chapter is divided into three main segments: Mixed Hi-Hat Patterns (single handed), Mixed Hi-Hat Patterns (with ghosted snare notes), and Mixed Hi-Hat/Snare Patterns (alternating sticking).

① Mixed Hi-Hat Patterns: **Single-Handed**

Mixing in 16th notes on the hi-hat pushes the beat forward.

Here's the basic framework beat:

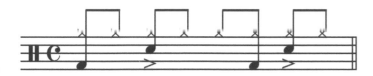

Here's that same beat with an extra hi-hat note on the "ah" of 2:

Track 91

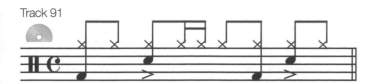

Play through both examples. Notice how adding a hi-hat note on the "ah" of 2 completely changes the feel and pushes the beat.

Here's a kick and snare pattern with steady eighth notes on the hi-hat:

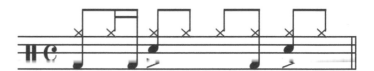

Now, here's that same kick and snare pattern with just two extra hi-hat notes added on the "ah" of 2 and the "e" of 3:

Track 92

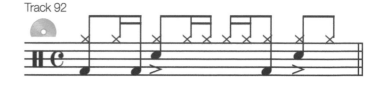

Again, notice how this pushes the beat. You can also add the open hi-hat to this concept:

Track 93

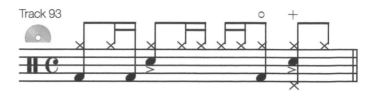

Using rests to break up the flow:

Here's a kick and snare pattern with steady eighth notes on the hi-hat:

Here's that same kick and snare pattern. The hi-hat pattern is broken up with an 8th-note rest on beat 3 of the measure: (Note: There's no hi-hat rest notated because the kick drum is still playing on beat 3.)

Track 94

Play through both of the previous examples. Notice how cutting out the hi-hat on beat 3 breaks up the flow of the beat. This is effective every once in a while. It will add more depth to your playing. Make sure you don't overuse this concept; and never sacrifice the groove or the pocket for the sake of switching up the beat.

You can also mix rests with 16th notes on the hi-hat. Here's a basic beat:

Here's the same kick and snare pattern. This time, the hi-hat pattern has extra 16th notes on the "ah" of 1 and the "e" of 2, and is broken up with a 16th-note rest on beat 2: (Note: There's no notated hi-hat rest because the snare is still playing on beat 2.)

Track 95

Play through both of the previous examples. Notice how cutting out the hi-hat breaks up the flow of the beat and makes it "sing." When you use this concept in your style, be sure to keep the hi-hat pattern in the pocket (don't rush or drag when the hi-hat drops out). Stay focused; don't let the underlying pulse of the beat waver.

"Footprints"
A Tribe Called Quest
People's Instinctive Travels and the Paths of Rhythm (Jive, 1990)

Check out the mixed hi-hat pattern, as well as the open hi-hat note on the "and" of 3.

♩ ≈100 bpm

▶ 0:38

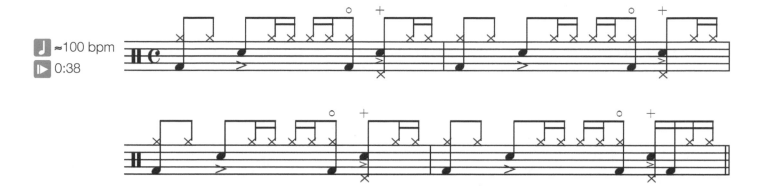

This song is based on a sample from **Donald Byrd's "Think Twice,"** off the album ***Stepping Into Tomorrow*** (Blue Note, 1975). Ali Shaheed Muhammad (the producer of "Footprints") added enhanced kick, snare, and hi-hat sounds to **Harvey Mason's** original drum pattern.

"Footsteps in the Dark"
The Isley Brothers
Go For Your Guns (T-Neck, 1977)

This song features **Ernie Isley** on drums. Notice how the hi-hat plays a combination of different 8th notes, 16th notes, and rests. This really makes the beat pop. Without this hi-hat part, the break, and the beat for the rest of the song, would be pretty basic and static. By mixing up the hi-hat pattern with 16th notes and rests, Ernie Isley created one of the most soulful drum breaks of all time.

♩ ≈81 bpm

▶ 0:00

This song was sampled for **Ice Cube**'s masterpiece **"It Was A Good Day,"** from the album ***The Predator*** (Priority, 1993). For this track, DJ Pooh (the producer) enhanced the original kick drum sound, and added a few extra kick drum notes.

2 Mixed Hi-Hat Patterns: **With Ghosted Snare Notes**

Here's the basic beat:

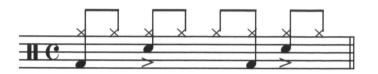

Here's that same kick/snare pattern with a mixed hi-hat pattern and ghosted snare notes. Make sure you blend the ghosted snare notes with the hi-hat:

Track 96

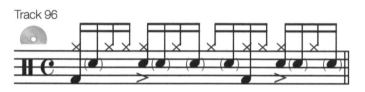

Play through both examples. Notice how this creates a steady stream of 16th notes and really fills out the beat.

This concept can have many of the same benefits as the Eighth Element—keeping steadier time, locking into a tight pocket, and creating a trance-like state for listeners and dancers.

This sometimes creates the phenomenon known as linear drumming (when only one component of the drumset is playing at a time). Here's an example of full-fledged linear drumming:

Track 97

Usually when combining mixed hi-hat patterns with ghosted snare notes, you'll find some instances of linear drumming; but it won't always create a full-on linear pattern.

For more information on linear drumming, check out the book *Linear Time Playing* (Alfred Publishing) by Gary Chaffee.

BREAKS

"Ebony Jam"
Tower of Power
In The Slot (Warner Bros., 1975)

This break features the great **David Garibaldi** on drums. Notice the hi-hat note on the "ah" of 4 in the second measure, leading into another on beat 1 as the measure is repeated. Also, check out the hi-hat rests on beats 2 and 4, and the ghosted snare notes on the "e" of 1, the "and" of 1, and the "and" of 4. Finally, notice how impeccably tight this break is.

≈113 bpm

0:00

This break was sampled for **De La Soul's "A Roller Skating Jam Named 'Saturdays',"** from the album ***De La Soul is Dead*** (Tommy Boy, 1991). Prince Paul (the producer of the track) took the second measure of the "Ebony Jam" break and looped it in order to make the "Saturdays" beat, arranging it so beat 3 of the "Ebony Jam" break becomes beat 1 of the "Saturdays" beat. He also added an open hi-hat note to the "ah" of 4 of the "Ebony" break (which is now the "ah" of 2 of the "Saturdays" beat).

③ Mixed Hi-Hat/Snare Patterns: **Alternating Sticking**

Here's a beat. Play the hi-hat pattern with one hand:

Track 98

R R R R L R R   R L R   L R R L

Now, here's the same beat. This time, use alternating sticking on the hi-hat:

Track 99

R L R L R L R   R L R   R L R L

Notice how the same beat can sound and feel completely different by switching up the sticking.

Alternating sticking is useful for playing "in-between-the-cracks" of straight and swung. Play the previous example beat with alternating sticking, and apply varying degrees of swing. A good way to do this is to start fully swung, then gradually morph to playing fully straight. Somewhere along the way you'll hit that "in-between-the-cracks" zone. Don't worry if you can't get this at first. Keep practicing and you'll eventually get it. Again, Stanton Moore's book *Groove Alchemy* has more information on this subject.

BEATS   **"Cissy Strut"**
The Meters
The Meters (Josie Records, 1969)

One of the most famous beats that incorporates a mixed hi-hat pattern with alternating sticking is "Cissy Strut" by The Meters, featuring the incomparable **Zigaboo Modeliste** on drums. Listen for how the drum groove is somewhere in between straight and swung.

♩≈88 bpm
▶ 0:03

L R L   R   L R L B   L R L   R   L R L B

This is just a suggested sticking. Use whatever works best for you. "Cissy Strut" was sampled for **"The Coolest,"** by **King Tee**, from the album ***Act a Fool*** (Capitol, 1988). DJ Pooh, the producer of the track, placed the sample on top of a programmed beat. However, you can still hear Zig in there.

Alternating sticking is also useful for performing the Ninth Element at higher tempos.

Let's use the previous example beat. Again, here it is:

R L R L R L R   R L R   R L R L

When you're comfortable with this beat, slowly increase the speed until you get to about 125 bpm. Notice how you can play the beat a lot faster if you use alternating sticking on the hi-hat (compared to playing the hi-hats with one hand). Most often, when dealing with quicker tempos, it's tighter to just keep steady 8th notes on the hi-hat and add sparse ghost notes on the snare. Use your discretion, and play whatever will best serve the situation at hand.

You can also apply alternating sticking to mixed hi-hat patterns with ghosted snare notes. When you utilize this concept, the right and left hands play on both the snare and the hi-hat.

Track 101

R L R L R L R L R L R   R L R L

You can use this concept at slower tempos to help you get that "in-between-the-cracks" feel. It's not only for faster tempos. You'll need to really refine your technique and feel in order to make this sound smooth and relaxed. This is an advanced concept, so it'll take more focused practice to get this down. (Note: Practicing pages 5-7 of *Stick Control*, by George Lawrence Stone, will help you with this.)

THE ARCHITECTS ::

ali shaheed muhammad

Ali Shaheed Muhammad was born on August 11, 1970 in Brooklyn, NY. He was raised in the Bedford Stuyvesant neighborhood, a.k.a. "Do or Die Bed Stuy." He became fascinated with music at a young age, to the point of carrying around a little yellow Mickey Mouse transistor radio wherever he went. His mother would often throw parties in their apartment, and his uncle would DJ them. At one of these parties, an eight-year-old Ali took control of the turntables and mixer, forever changing his life. He rose through the ranks of the local neighborhood DJs and eventually formed the legendary A Tribe Called Quest along with Phife Dawg and Q-Tip. Ali drew from an extensive knowledge of music to find samples. He combined these samples in a profoundly innovative manner to create Tribe's beats. They released five critically-acclaimed albums from 1990 to 1998, then disbanded at their peak due to personality conflicts. Ali was also a member of the music collective The Ummah (which means "community"). This collective featured Q-Tip along with superstar producer J. Dilla. They produced tracks for Busta Rhymes, Keith Murray, and The Brand New Heavies, among many others. After Tribe broke up, Ali went on to form Lucy Pearl with Dawn Robinson and Raphael Saadiq. In addition to hip-hop, the group explored funk, rock, and R&B. In 2004, he released his first solo album, *Shaheedullah and Stereotypes* (Garden Seeker Productions/Penalty Recordings). This album veers away from Ali's earlier sample-heavy work and features more live instrumentation. His beliefs as a Muslim surface on the album. "Shaheedullah," which means "witness to God," was intended to be Ali's middle name. However, his mother thought it was too long and shortened it to Shaheed. Ali is well aware of the negative stereotypes Muslims receive today, hence the title of his first solo album. Ali Shaheed Muhammad took the torch from the early breakbeat DJs, and helped advance the art form. He's still blazing a path and taking it to the next level today. (www.giantstep.net)

Mixed Hi-Hat Patterns (Single-Handed): **Exercises**

The kick and snare patterns are basic, and are the same for each exercise. This will allow you to focus on the more intricate hi-hat patterns. You can also play the rhythms from *Syncopation* (by Ted Reed) on the hi-hat, over the kick/snare pattern from these exercises. Start slow and gradually increase the tempo.

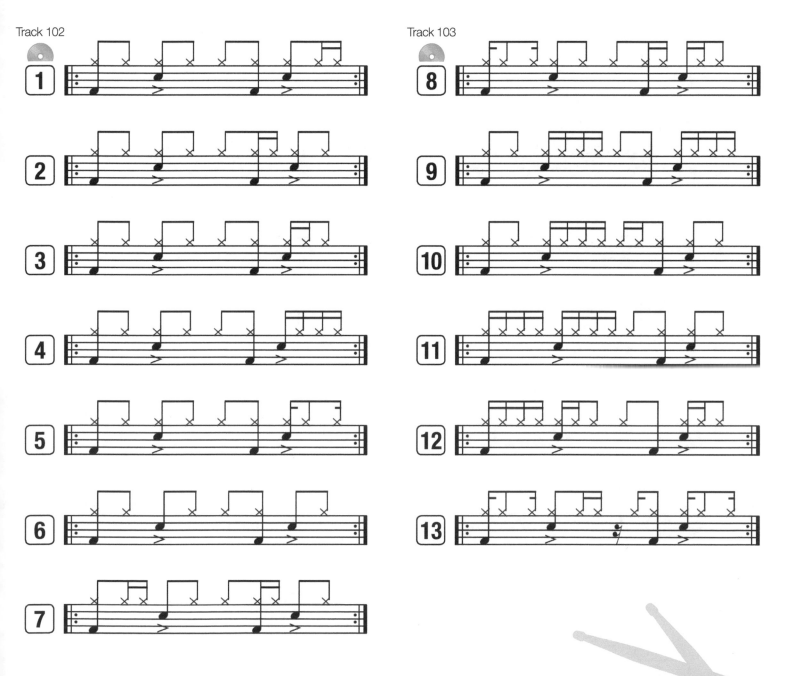

Mixed Hi-Hat Patterns (Single-Handed): **Beats**

These beats feature mixed hi-hat patterns. The kick and snare patterns are basic so you can focus on the more intricate hi-hat patterns. Remember to start slow and gradually increase the tempo. Feel free to play around with the swing of the hi-hat patterns. You can also switch up your hands when you practice these beats (left hand plays the hi-hat, right hand plays the snare—opposite for lefties). This will help your coordination and strengthen your weaker hand.

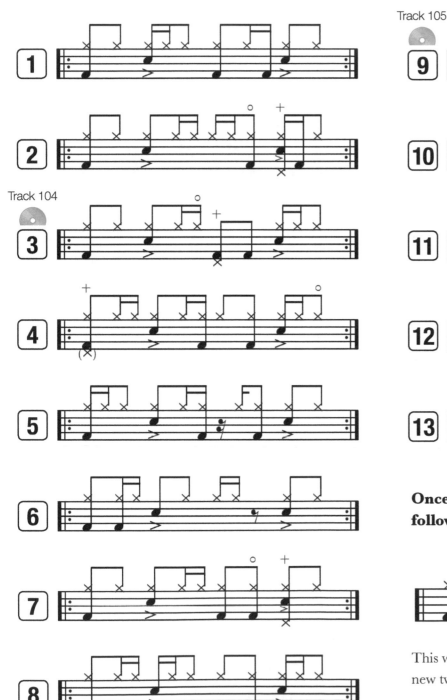

Track 104

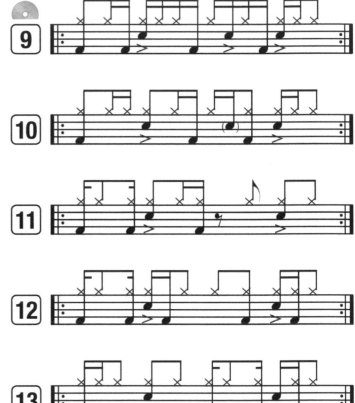

Track 105

Once you're comfortable with these beats, play th[e] following beat before each of them:

This will make each beat into a two-bar phrase. Repeat each new two-bar phrase 20 times, then move on to the next one.

Mixed Hi-Hat Patterns (with Ghosted Snare Notes):
Exercises

These exercises apply various paradiddle combinations between the snare and hi-hat over basic kick drum patterns. This will help you get comfortable mixing broken hi-hat patterns with ghosted snare notes. Start slow (60 bpm) and gradually increase the tempo. This will help you get an even, relaxed flow happening with the exercises. Remember to record yourself and analyze the playback. Make sure you blend the ghosted snare notes with the hi-hat patterns. (Note: Practicing pages 5-7 of *Stick Control* will help you perform these exercises at a higher level.)

Track 106

Track 107

Mixed Hi-Hat Patterns (with Ghosted Snare Notes): **Beats**

These beats feature mixed hi-hat patterns with ghosted snare notes. Look out for some examples of linear drumming within these beats. Make sure the hi-hat and snare notes are evenly spaced (you don't want to squeeze them together). Record yourself and analyze the playback. Start slow and get a smooth feel happening before you increase the tempo. Make sure the ghosted snare notes are blended with the hi-hat patterns. (Note: Don't forget to practice *Stick Control* in conjunction with these beats.)

Once you're comfortable with these beats, play the following beat before each of them:

This will make each beat into a two-bar phrase. Repeat each new two-bar phrase 20 times, then move on to the next one.

Mixed Hi-Hat/Snare Patterns (Alternating Sticking):
Exercises

These exercises feature mixed hi-hat/snare patterns with alternating sticking, played over basic kick drum patterns. This will help you get comfortable with the concept, and allow you to smoothly blend it into your style. Start slow and gradually increase the tempo.

Exercises 10-13 are a bit more advanced; take these extra slow at first.

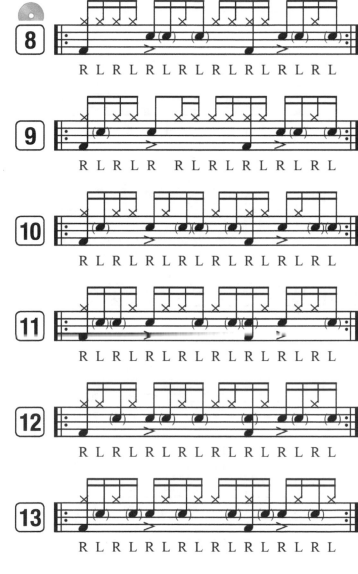

Mixed Hi-Hat/Snare Patterns (Alternating Sticking): **Beats**

These beats feature alternating sticking applied to various hi-hat/snare patterns.
Experiment with varying degrees of swing as you practice/play these beats.
Use them as a vehicle to get in-between-the-cracks of straight and swung.
Record yourself and analyze the playback. Be sure to start slowly and get
a relaxed, controlled groove happening.

Once you're comfortable with these beats, play the following beat before each of them:

This will make each beat into a two-bar phrase. Repeat each
new two-bar phrase 20 times, then move on to the next one.

Track 112

Track 113

Mixed Hi-Hat Patterns: **8-Bar Phrase**

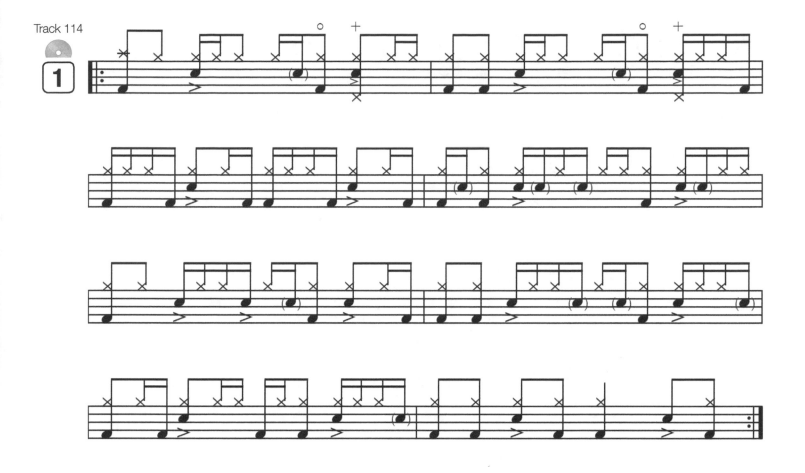

When you're comfortable with the eight-bar phrase, apply it to the following grid:

Groove   8-Bar Phrase

For the initial eight bars of groove, use any beat from the chapter, or make up your own.

Mixed Hi-Hat Patterns: **8-Bar Phrase**

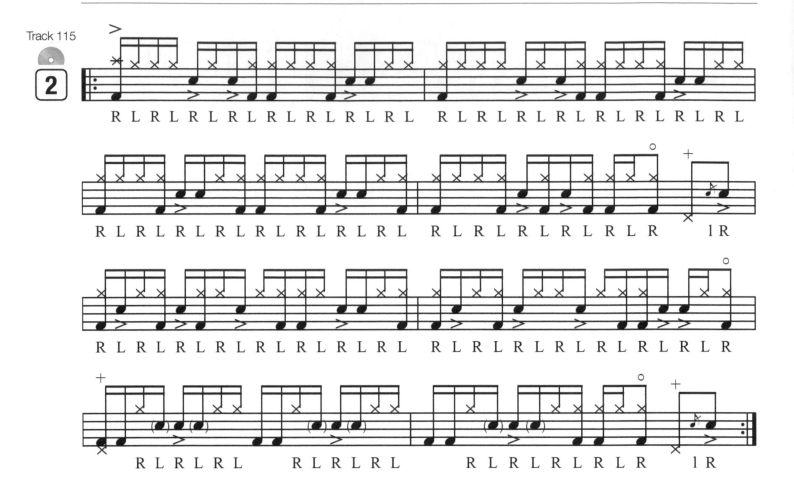

R L R L R L R L R L R L R L R L   R L R L R L R L R L R L R L R L

R L R L R L R L R L R L R L R L   R L R L R L R L R L R L R   1 R

R L R L R L R L R L R L R L R L   R L R L R L R L R L R L R L R L R

R L R L R L   R L R L R L   R L R L R L R L R   1 R

When you're comfortable with the eight-bar phrase, apply it to the following grid:

Groove   8-Bar Phrase

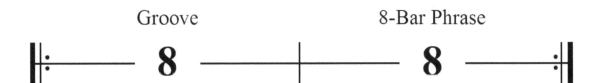

For the initial eight bars of groove, use any beat from the chapter, or make up your own.

e10
The Tenth Element
The kick drum playing more than two 16th notes in a row.

This usually occurs as three 16th notes in a row (but can be more). In addition to creating power, drive, and weight, this can also determine the swing of the beat. The Tenth Element is used sparsely in breakbeat drumming, usually at tempos of 100 bpm or slower. This element is most authentically performed with a single kick pedal (a double pedal won't quite provide that classic feel).

There are four different ways this element can appear, depending on where the first of the three 16th notes is started.

Either the "1-e-and," "2-e-and," "3-e-and," or "4-e-and":

Any of the "e-and-ah's" of the beat:

Either the "and-ah-1," "and-ah-2," "and-ah-3," or "and-ah-4":

Either the "ah-1-e," "ah-2-e," "ah-3-e," or "ah-4-e":

Let's compare the four different variations of the Tenth Element with a basic beat.

① Kick drum on the "1-e-and":

Here's a basic beat:

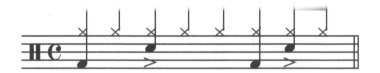

Now we'll add three 16th notes in a row on the kick (on the "1-e-and"):

Track 116

Play through both examples. Notice how starting the three sixteenth notes on beat 1 adds power to the beat. It also creates movement by "pushing" the beat along.

② Kick drum on the "e-and-ah":

Again, here's a basic beat:

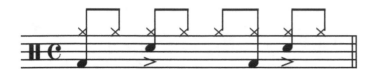

Now we'll add three 16th notes in a row on the kick (on the "e-and-ah" of beat 3):

Track 117

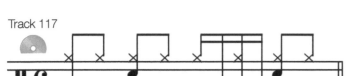

Play through both examples. Notice how starting the three sixteenth notes in a row on the "e" adds drive to the beat. This time, the movement is created by "pulling" the beat along.

③ Kick drum on the "and-ah-3":

Again, the basic beat:

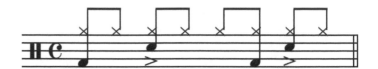

Now we'll add three 16th notes in a row on the kick (on the "and-ah-3"):

Track 118

Play both example beats. Notice how starting the three sixteenth notes in a row on the "and" doesn't create as much movement. It does, however, add "weight" to the beat.

④ Kick drum on the "ah-3-e":

The basic beat:

Now we'll add three 16th notes in a row on the kick (on the "ah-3-e"):

Track 119

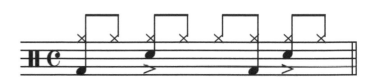

Notice how starting the three sixteenth notes in a row on the "ah" adds drive and helps propel the beat.

"Synthetic Substitution"
Melvin Bliss
released as a single (Sunburst, 1973)

The break occurs at the beginning of the song. It features the Tenth Element in the third beat of each measure.

♩ ≈93 bpm

▶ 0:00

This break was sampled for the **Dr. Octagon** song **"Wild and Crazy,"** from the album **Dr. Octagoneocologyst** (Mo Wax, 1996). Dan The Automator (the producer) enhanced the original kick drum sound.

You can also play more than three 16th notes in a row on the kick drum.

"Night of the Living Baseheads"
Public Enemy
It Takes a Nation of Millions to Hold Us Back (Def Jam, 1988)

Notice the five 16th notes in a row on the kick in the second bar. This beat is based on a sample from **"Do the Funky Penguin,"** by **Rufus Thomas** (see page 144 of the Breakbeat Transcriptions chapter). Hank Shocklee (the producer) chopped up the "Funky Penguin" break and added extra kick, snare, and hi-hat notes. The "Night of the Living Baseheads" beat is an eight-bar phrase. Here are the 5th and 6th bars:

♩ ≈106 bpm

▶ 1:18

"Ain't Sayin Nothin New"
The Roots
Things Fall Apart (MCA Records, 1999)

Notice the four 16th notes in row on the kick drum beginning on beat 1 and continuing to the "ah" of 1. Listen to the slight swing that **Questlove** puts on these 16th notes. This makes the beat bounce and gives it that "head nod" factor.

♩ ≈93 bpm

▶ 0:00

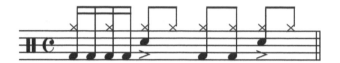

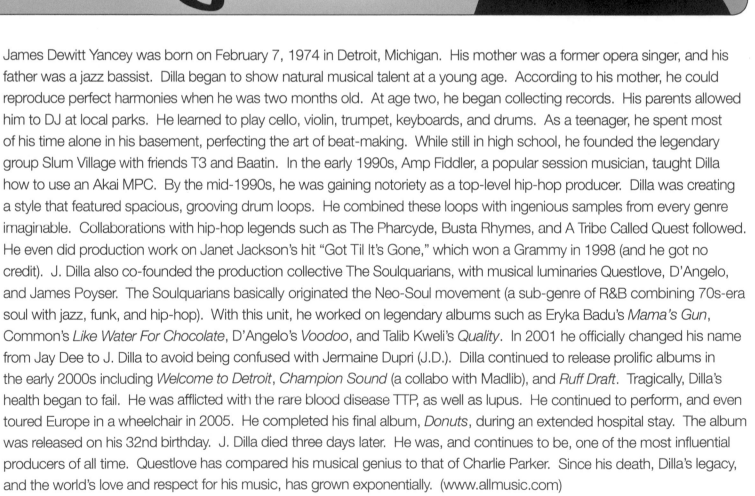

THE ARCHITECTS :: j dilla

James Dewitt Yancey was born on February 7, 1974 in Detroit, Michigan. His mother was a former opera singer, and his father was a jazz bassist. Dilla began to show natural musical talent at a young age. According to his mother, he could reproduce perfect harmonies when he was two months old. At age two, he began collecting records. His parents allowed him to DJ at local parks. He learned to play cello, violin, trumpet, keyboards, and drums. As a teenager, he spent most of his time alone in his basement, perfecting the art of beat-making. While still in high school, he founded the legendary group Slum Village with friends T3 and Baatin. In the early 1990s, Amp Fiddler, a popular session musician, taught Dilla how to use an Akai MPC. By the mid-1990s, he was gaining notoriety as a top-level hip-hop producer. Dilla was creating a style that featured spacious, grooving drum loops. He combined these loops with ingenious samples from every genre imaginable. Collaborations with hip-hop legends such as The Pharcyde, Busta Rhymes, and A Tribe Called Quest followed. He even did production work on Janet Jackson's hit "Got Til It's Gone," which won a Grammy in 1998 (and he got no credit). J. Dilla also co-founded the production collective The Soulquarians, with musical luminaries Questlove, D'Angelo, and James Poyser. The Soulquarians basically originated the Neo-Soul movement (a sub-genre of R&B combining 70s-era soul with jazz, funk, and hip-hop). With this unit, he worked on legendary albums such as Eryka Badu's *Mama's Gun*, Common's *Like Water For Chocolate*, D'Angelo's *Voodoo*, and Talib Kweli's *Quality*. In 2001 he officially changed his name from Jay Dee to J. Dilla to avoid being confused with Jermaine Dupri (J.D.). Dilla continued to release prolific albums in the early 2000s including *Welcome to Detroit*, *Champion Sound* (a collabo with Madlib), and *Ruff Draft*. Tragically, Dilla's health began to fail. He was afflicted with the rare blood disease TTP, as well as lupus. He continued to perform, and even toured Europe in a wheelchair in 2005. He completed his final album, *Donuts*, during an extended hospital stay. The album was released on his 32nd birthday. J. Dilla died three days later. He was, and continues to be, one of the most influential producers of all time. Questlove has compared his musical genius to that of Charlie Parker. Since his death, Dilla's legacy, and the world's love and respect for his music, has grown exponentially. (www.allmusic.com)

Three 16th Notes in a Row on the Kick: **Exercises**

These exercises will help you play three 16th notes in a row on the kick drum. It's important to start these exercises slow, so you can get a controlled flow happening. If you go too fast too soon, you won't develop the necessary muscles (and your kick drum notes won't be as tight and smooth as they could be). After you get comfortable with these, you can add the snare on 2 and 4 (or on 1, 2, 3, and 4). It will take a while to build up your kick drum speed for this element. Remember: it's important to gradually develop the muscles over a longer period of time. This will eventually enable you to play faster and smoother.

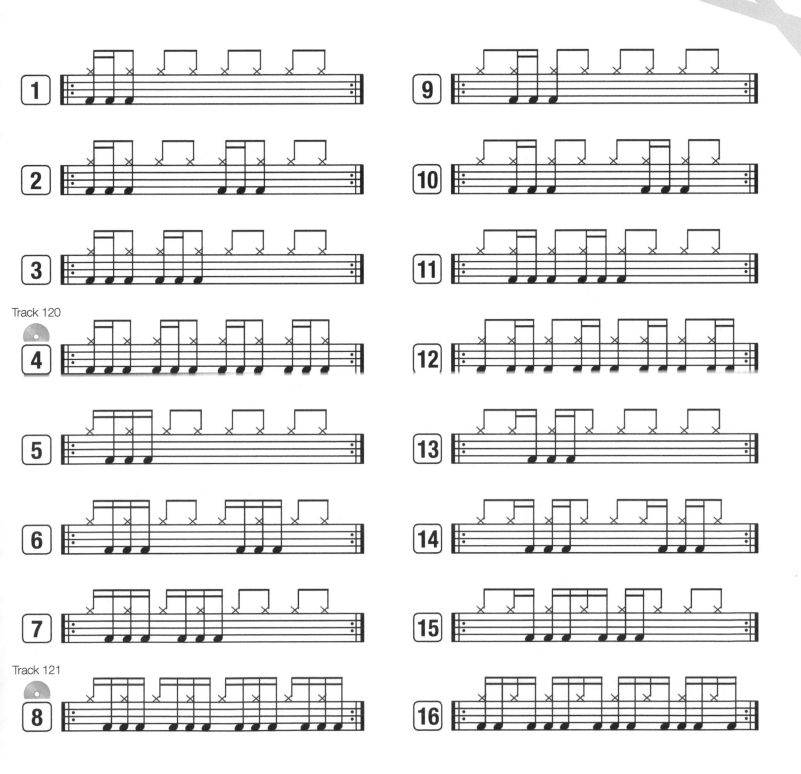

Track 120

Track 121

These beats feature three 16th notes in a row on the kick drum. Again, start these beats slow (60 bpm), and gradually increase the tempo. When practicing/playing these beats, focus on finding a well-balanced body position. Search for that sweet spot, where your kick drum leg is kind of suspended; your foot, ankle, and calf are doing most of the work. Keep searching for that zone where everything just falls into place. You can't force it, it just has to happen. Also, make sure you don't put too much weight on your hi-hat foot. Stay balanced. Don't forget to record yourself and listen to the playback.

When you're comfortable with the Tenth Element beats, play the following beat before each of them:

This will make each beat into a two-bar phrase. Play each new two-bar phrase 20 times, then move on to the next one.

Three 16th Notes in a Row on the Kick: **8-Bar Phrase**

Track 124

When you're comfortable with the eight bar phrase, apply it to the following grid.

Groove   8-Bar Phrase

8   8

For the initial eight bars of groove, use any beat from the chapter, or make up your own.

The Eleventh Element
Broken 16th-note triplets played on the kick and/or snare.

In addition to adding style to a beat, this element also creates bounce. It's pretty flashy, so you can use it to draw attention to your playing. This is another element that's used sparsely in breakbeat drumming. The less you use it, the more effective it'll be when you do use it. This element is most authentically replicated with a single kick drum pedal. It gives it that "classic" old-school feel.

Before we get into this element, let's look at the 16th-note triplet.

Each eighth note in a measure of 4/4 can be divided into three 16th-note triplets.

16th-note triplets are connected with a double bar and usually have the number "3" above them.

Therefore, one beat of two eighth notes will contain six 16th-note triplets.

If there's six in a row they usually have the number "6" over them.

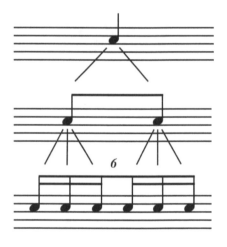

A full measure of 4/4 time contains twenty-four 16th-note triplets. They're counted "1-trip-let-and-trip-let 2-trip-let-and-trip-let 3-trip-let-and-trip-let 4-trip-let-and-trip-let":

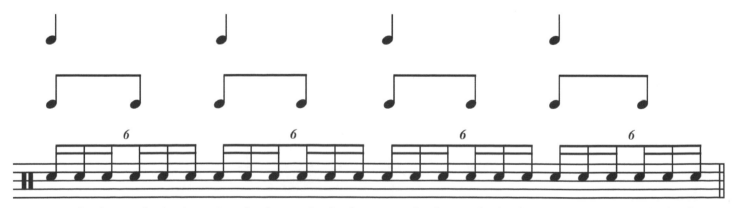

1 trip let and trip let   2 trip let and trip let   3 trip let and trip let   4 trip let and trip let

When applied to breakbeats, 16th-note triplets are often played two at a time, on either the kick or snare. This is where the term "broken" comes from, because the group of three triplets is broken up into a group of two. They're usually "sandwiched" between two eighth notes on the hi-hat.

This is what the broken 16th-note triplets look like when played on the snare:

This is what they look like when played on the kick:

Applying the Eleventh Element to Beats

Broken 16th-note triplets on the kick applied to a beat:

In this example, the kick is playing on beat 1, and on the last two 16th-note triplets (the "trip-let") of beat three:

Track 125

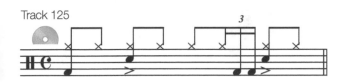

Notice the bounce this adds to the beat.

Broken 16th-note triplets on the snare applied to a beat:

Broken 16th-note triplets on the snare are usually either ghosted or played mezzo forte.

Ghosted:

In this example, the snare plays ghost notes on the second and third 16th-note triplets (the "trip-let") of beat 3:

Track 126

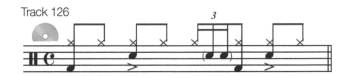

Again, notice the bounce and extra style this creates.

Mezzo Forte: (medium loud)

In this example, the snare plays mezzo forte notes on the second and third 16th-note triplets (the "trip-let") of beat 3:

Track 127

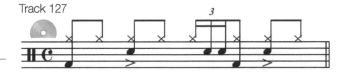

It's sometimes more effective to play the broken 16th-note triplets on the snare at a mezzo forte level, instead of ghosted.

Broken 16th-note triplets on both the kick and snare:

In this example, the kick plays the last two 16th-note triplets of beat 1, and the snare plays the last two 16th-note triplets of beat 2:

Track 128

Using the broken 16th-note triplets on both the kick and snare will add more style to your beat. Remember, you don't want to overuse this element.

"Can We Rap"
Carleen and the Groovers
Can We Rap [Now-Again Records, 2004 (reissue)]

This break features **Carleen Jean Butler** on drums. The song was originally released around 1972, but was reissued by Now-Again Records in 2004. The break features broken 16th-note triplets on the kick drum. The broken 16th-note triplets occur in the first and third measures. Be sure to listen to this one; it's a tight break and a great song.

♩ ≈117 bpm
▶ 0:55

THE ARCHITECTS ::
afrika bambaataa

Afrika Bambaataa was born on October 4, 1960. He's known as the "Grandfather," "Godfather," and the "Amen Ra" of hip-hop. He grew up in the Bronx River Projects, raised by his mother and uncle. Growing up, he was exposed to his mother's extensive record collection. In the Bronx during the 1970s, most kids joined gangs for protection. As a teenager, Bambaataa joined The Savage Seven gang, which later became the Black Spades. His charisma and leadership skills helped him expand his gang's turf and membership numbers. Soon, the Black Spades were the biggest gang in the Bronx. In high school, Bambaataa won an essay contest, and his prize was a trip to Africa. The communities he visited in Africa inspired him to get away from violence. He began working to create a peaceful community in his neighborhood. Upon returning to America, he founded the Universal Zulu Nation, a collective of socially and politically aware youths. The goal of the Zulu Nation was to build a positive social movement.

As a teenager, Bam was an avid record collector and began DJing house parties in the Bronx. He was known as "Master of Records," because of the variety he brought to the turntables. He mixed genres such as go-go, salsa, soca, reggae, jazz, funk, and World. He's credited with introducing songs such as "Jam on the Groove" and "Calypso Breakdown" by Ralph McDonald, "Dance to the Drummer's Beat" by Herman Kelly, and "Trans-Europe Express" by Kaftwerk to the hip-hop world. Mix tapes of Bam's parties often sold for as much as $40. Bambaataa went on to form the legendary Soulsonic Force, a collective of Zulu Nation members that he records and performs with to this day.

Afrika Bambaataa is actually credited with naming hip-hop. He began using the term when referring to the emerging culture which included the music of DJs, the lyrics and poetry of MCs, breakdancing, graffiti, and knowledge. Bambaataa was able to use his charisma and leadership skills to spread hip-hop through house parties, block parties, gym dances, and mix tapes. Bam released his first singles in 1980: "Death Mix" and "Zulu Nation Throwdown." In 1982, he took a crew out for the first overseas hip-hop tour of Europe. Overseas touring would help hip-hop become a global culture. He also released the pivotal album, *Planet Rock*. It featured the single "Planet Rock," which was based on "Trans-Europe Express" by Kraftwerk. The record pioneered the Electro-Funk sound, and went gold. In the same year, Bambaataa performed at the legendary Mudd Club in NYC; his first performance for a predominantly white audience. The white folks loved it, and his crowds steadily grew larger.

In 1984, Bam teamed up with the legendary James Brown to create the landmark album *Unity*.

Bambaataa continued with social and political activism. His single "Self Destruction" helped raise $400,000.00 for the National Urban League's anti violence campaign. He also worked on an anti-apartheid album called *Sun City*, which featured Lou Reed, Joey Ramone, Steve Van Zandt, and U2.

Bam founded his own record label in 1992, Planet Rock Records. In 1994 he began DJing on Hot 97 in NYC, with a show called True School at Noon. Afrika Bambaataa helped crystallize hip-hop and bring it, along with his message of peace, unity, love, and having fun to the masses. (www.zulunation.com) (www.rollingstone.com)

Broken 16th-Note Triplets on the Kick and/or Snare: **Exercises**

These exercises will help you play broken 16th-note triplets on the kick and snare. Use these to really focus on the execution of your broken 16th-note triplets—strive for the highest possible level of performance. Remember to start slow so you can get an even, relaxed feel happening. Gradually increase the tempo. At first, it might be difficult to pull off two 16th-note triplets in a row with a single kick pedal. Play the first of the two notes with your toe further down on the pedal. Then, after the first note is played, slide your foot up towards the front of the pedal to play the second note. This will help you play those two notes in a row with a little extra speed and fluidity. Again, you just have to spend some time and experiment to get into that zone. This is something that you can't force. Keep practicing, and it'll eventually fall into place. (Note: Also, practice these exercises with the snare notes ghosted.)

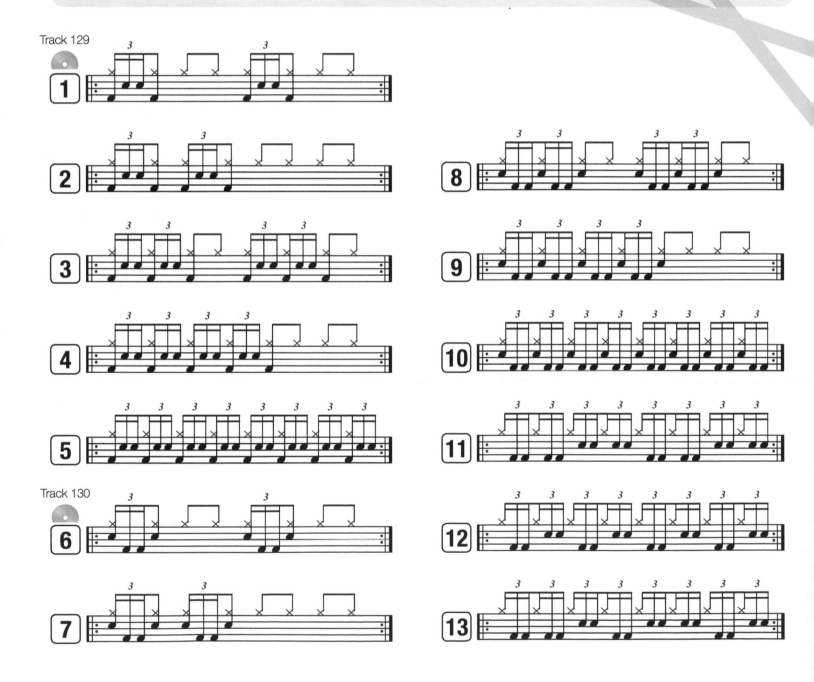

Broken 16th-Note Triplets on the Kick and/or Snare:
Beats

It's important to start these beats slowly (60 bpm) and gradually increase the tempo. Strive for a clean performance of the broken 16th-note triplets. Make sure they blend smoothly with the rest of the beat. Pay attention to the hi-hat pattern, making sure the eighth notes are evenly spaced. Don't stretch some of them in order to accommodate the 16th-note triplets. Keep the tempo down until you get everything sounding smooth.

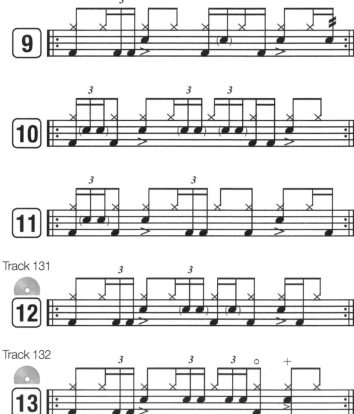

Once you're comfortable with the Eleventh Element beats, play the following beat before each of them:

This will make each beat into a two-bar phrase. Play each new two-bar phrase 20 times, then move on to the next one.

Broken 16th-Note Triplets on the Kick and/or Snare:
8-Bar Phrase

When you're comfortable with the eight-bar phrase, apply it to the following grid:

Groove   8-Bar Phrase

For the initial eight bars of groove, use any beat from the chapter, or make up your own.

The Twelfth Element
Unison drumming (sometimes referred to as chordal drumming).

There are two main aspects to this element. The first aspect occurs when two or more components of the drumset play a unison phrase. This means that the sound sources, let's say the kick and the hi-hat, are playing the same rhythmic pattern at the same time. This adds texture and reinforces a rhythmic phrase. The second aspect of this element occurs when two or more components, let's say the kick, snare, and hi-hat, play a unison accent. This is a good way to add weight and color to an accented note. It's also a powerful way to begin or end a phrase. The Twelfth Element is one of the more technically advanced elements.

Don't confuse the Twelfth Element with the hi-hat and snare, or the hi-hat and kick, playing at the same time during a beat. This is a natural occurrence when a beat is played on the drumset:

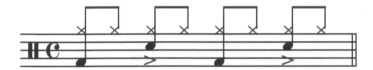

Unison Phrases

Here's a two bar beat that features the kick drum and hi-hat playing a unison phrase:

Track 134

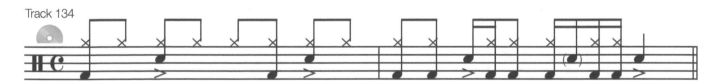

Notice how in the first bar, the hi-hat and kick play at the same time, as do the hi-hat and snare. This is just part of the beat. However, in the second bar, the hi-hat and kick join forces for a unison phrase. Having both the kick and hi-hat play that rhythmic phrase adds texture and helps reinforce the pattern.

In a regular beat, the different sound sources are not joining forces for a unison phrase, as they are in the second bar of the above example.

"Can We Rap"

Carleen and the Groovers

Can We Rap [Now-Again Records, 2004 (reissue)]

Let's revisit the "Can We Rap" break. The fourth bar of this break contains a good example of unison drumming. Check out the unison pattern between the ride cymbal and kick drum:

Unison Accents

Here's a two-bar beat. The first bar is basic. The second features the kick, snare, and open hi-hat playing a unison accent on the "and" of 3:

Track 135

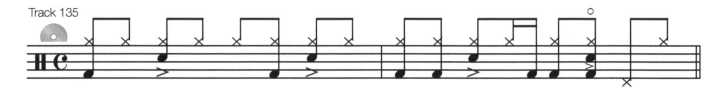

Notice how this really makes the accent pop out. There is no way anyone is not gonna hear and feel that "and" of 3 in the second bar.

The Twelfth Element can also be subtly applied to beats. Here's a one-bar beat that features the Twelfth Element:

Track 136

Notice the ghosted snare and kick on the "e" of two as well as the "and" of three.

Zigaboo Modeliste of The Meters is a master of this element. It plays a huge role in his style, which leads us to...

"Look-ka Py Py"
The Meters
Look-ka Py Py (Josie Records, 1969)

This break features the great **Zigaboo Modeliste** on drums. The kick, snare, and open hi-hat play a unison accent on the "and" of 3 in both measures of this two bar break. This is a *ridiculously* funky break.

"Foodstamps"
24 Carat Black
Ghetto: Misfortune's Wealth (Enterprise, 1973)

This break features **Tyrone Steele** on drums. The break occurs at the beginning of the song. It features the kick, rim click, and half-open hi-hat accenting on the "and" of 2. This break is also a great example of the power of repetition.

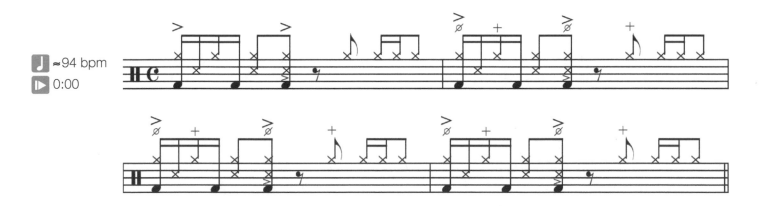

This break was sampled for the **Digable Planet's** song **"Rebirth of Slick (Cool Like Dat)"** from the album **Reachin (A New Refutation of Time and Space)** (Pendulum, 1993). Butterfly, the producer of the track, used the "Foodstamps" break only twice in the song (for one measure at a time). One measure of the break appears at 2:28, and again at 3:28. For the main beat of the song, he used a chopped up and enhanced version of the "Impeach the President" break (discussed in the Fifth Element chapter of this book).

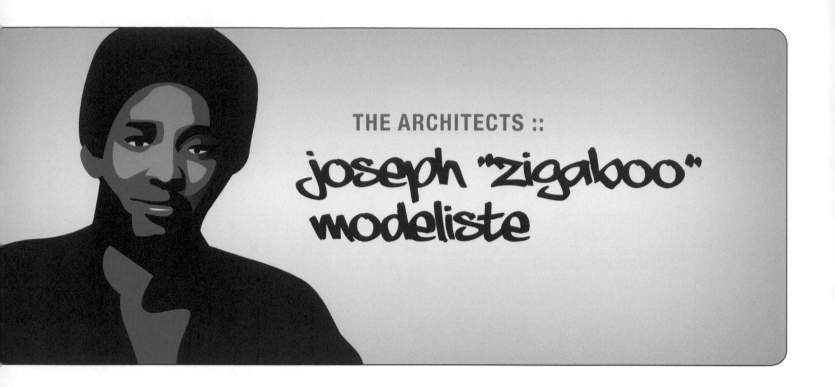

joseph "zigaboo" modeliste

Zigaboo was born on December 28, 1948 in New Orleans, Louisiana. For the past thirty-plus years he's been an endless source of funk influence for musicians, producers, and DJs. He began his career drumming for musical legend Fats Domino. In 1967, Zig co-founded The Meters, a legendary New Orleans funk band. This group was the in-house studio band for Allen Toussaint's record label, Sansu Enterprises. They backed legendary artists including Robert Palmer, Dr. John, and Paul McCartney. The Meters also recorded a vast catalog of original material while creating and innovating funk. The group disbanded in 1979, and Zig went on to back some of the biggest names of the day, including Keith Richards and his New Barbarians project. Most recently, the master drummer has formulated projects such as Zigaboo Modeliste and the New Aahkesstra, and Zigaboo's Funk Revue. In addition, he reunites with The Meters for an occasional show. Zig's drumming style is deep, completely original, and instantly recognizable. He mixes the straight-ahead pulse of R&B with the syncopated beats of New Orleans Second Line brass bands. One aspect of his style is loose and linear (only one component of the drumset plays at a time). The other aspect is chordal (multiple components of the drumset are played in unison). His beats have been sampled by artists such as Ice Cube, A Tribe Called Quest, and Digable Planets, among hundreds of others. His style prevails in contemporary music, and provides a natural, organic swing in this digital age of sampling and beat programming. Public Enemy's Hank Shocklee, one of the founding fathers of hip-hop, refers to Zig's drumming as "...the formula for funk and hip-hop as we know it." (www.zigaboo.com) (www.drummagazine.com) (www.themetersonline.com)

Unison/Chordal Drumming: **Exercises**

These exercises will help you play multiple sound sources in unison. For most drummers, playing unison phrases between the right hand and kick drum is pretty natural. However, playing left-hand and kick unisons is usually a bit awkward at first. Playing left-hand and right-hand unisons is also a bit unnatural at first. Playing left-hand, right-hand, and foot unisons will require some extra practice as well. Remember to start slow and record yourself. Make sure you're not flamming the unisons, and that everything is nice and tight. Practice these with the snare notes ghosted as well as accented. You can also practice the rhythms from *Syncopation*, by Ted Reed, with kick/snare/hi-hat unisons.

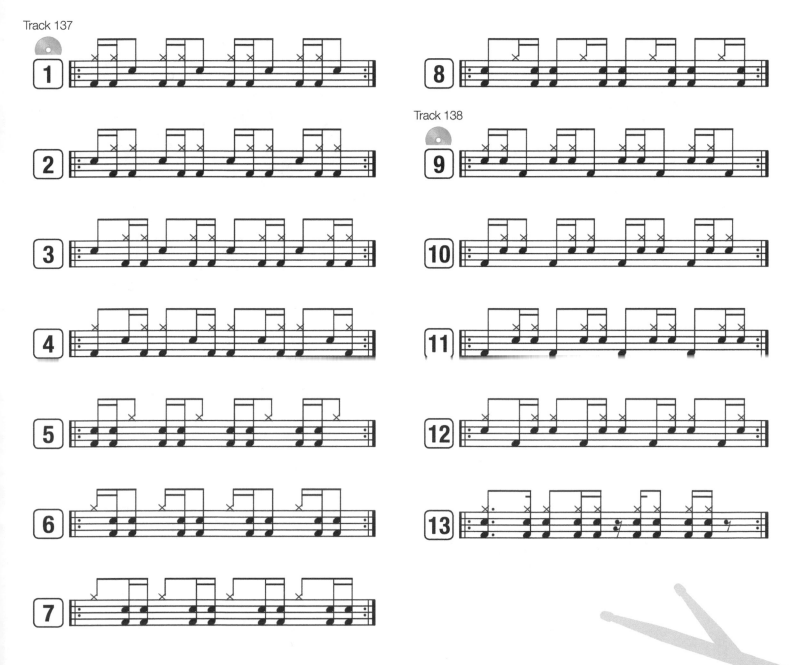

These beats feature chordal-style drumming. Make sure you start slow. As you're playing, it may feel like everything is smooth. Record yourself to make sure this is the case. If not, don't worry. Keep practicing and it'll smooth out. Many of these beats can also be used as fills, like how Butterfly used the "Foodstamps" break in "Rebirth of Slick" (see page 107).

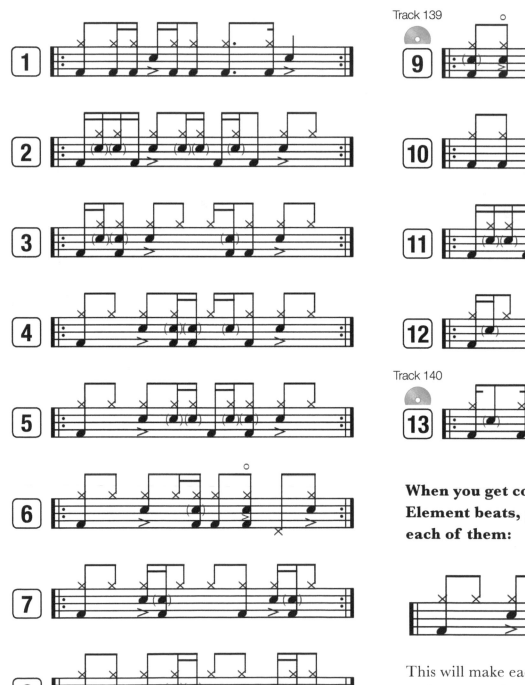

Track 139

Track 140

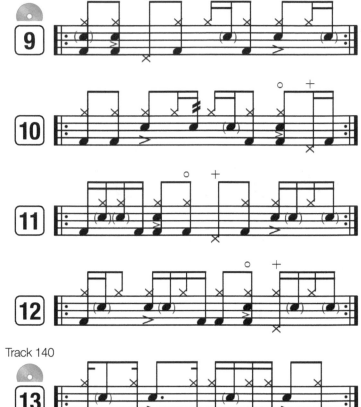

When you get comfortable with the Twelfth Element beats, play the following beat before each of them:

This will make each beat into a two-bar phrase. Play each new two-bar phrase 20 times, then move on to the next one.

Unison/Chordal Drumming: **8-Bar Phrase**

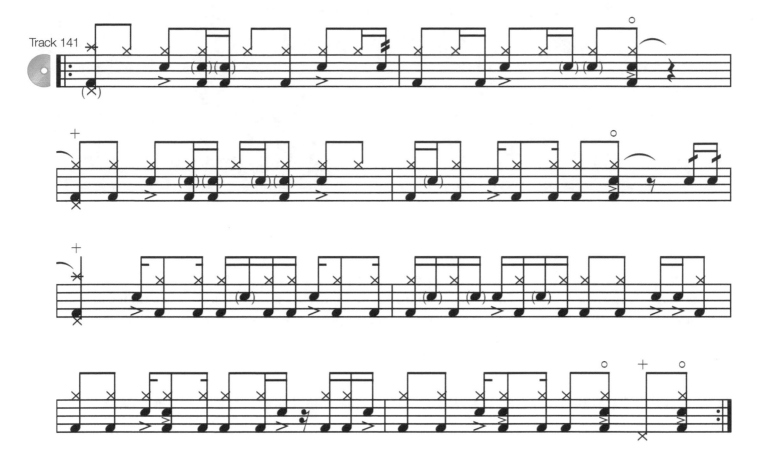

Track 141

When you're comfortable with the eight bar phrase, apply it to the following grid.

Groove   8-Bar Phrase

For the initial eight bars of groove, use any beat from the chapter, or make up your own.

The Thirteenth Element
Superimposing a three-16th-note phrase, played between the kick and snare, over 4/4 time.

This element creates a polyrhythmic 3-over-2 feeling. Since the pulse of the beat is slightly disguised by the polyrhythmic feel, the Thirteenth Element adds tension to a beat. The three-16th-note phrases can occur in the following combinations: one kick note and two snare notes, one snare note and two kick notes, or one kick note, one snare note and a 16th note rest. The kick/snare combinations can occur in any order. For example, let's say the phrase consists of one kick note and two snare notes. These can occur as "kick-snare-snare," "snare-snare-kick," or "snare-kick-snare." The manner in which these different phrases and combinations are applied to breakbeat drumming is wide open to the stylistic interpretations of the drummer.

Let's look at the three main combinations of this element:

1 Here's what a three-16th-note phrase consisting of one kick note and two snare notes looks like through a measure of 4/4:

Notice the rhythm created by the kick drum. This helps define the underlying polyrhythmic feel of the phrase.

2 Here's what a three-16th-note phrase of one snare note and two kick notes looks like:

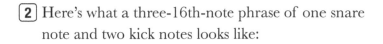

Notice the rhythm created by the snare. Again, this helps define the underlying polyrhythmic feeling of the phrase.

3 Here's what one kick note, one snare note, and a 16th-note rest looks like:

Notice the extra space this combination creates. This is a good way to apply the Thirteenth Element without using too many notes and playing too busily.

Applying the Thirteenth Element to Beats

This example is a two-bar beat. The first bar is basic, while the second bar features a three-16th-note phrase of one kick note and two snare notes played through the measure:

Track 142

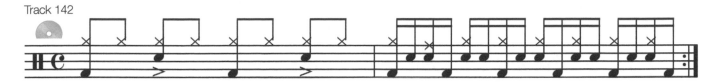

Notice the tension that's created in the second bar, and the release when you come back around to the first bar.

Here's another two-bar beat. The first bar is basic, while the second bar features a three-16th-note phrase of one snare note and two kick notes played through the measure:

Track 143

Again, notice the tension and release.

Here's another two-bar beat. The second bar of this example contains a three-16th-note phrase of one snare note, one kick note, and a 16th-note rest:

Track 144

Although the kick and snare are resting as the third note of the three-note phrase, the hi-hat does "fill in the holes" on the "and" of 1, beat 3, and the "and" of 4. Notice how the tension and release is still created, but there's also some space.

You can also play the three-16th-note phrase for half of a measure:

Track 145

Applying accents and ghost notes to this concept adds another layer of texture:

Track 146

BREAKS

"Give it Up"
Kool and the Gang
Kool and the Gang (De-Lite Records, 1969)

This break features the great **George Brown** on drums. The use of the Thirteenth Element begins on the "ah" of 4 in the third bar, and continues until the "e" of 3 in the fourth bar. Notice the space, but also the tension this creates. The tension is then resolved in the next bar of the song as the rest of the band comes back in. The break occurs at 1:36. (Note: "Give It Up" also features notable drum breaks at 1:11, 2:01, and 3:01)

♩ ≈98 bpm
▶ 1:36

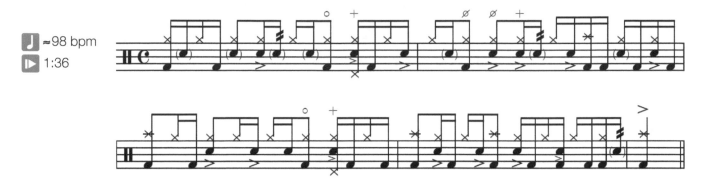

The drums from this break, as well as a few horn lines from the song, were sampled for **Eric B. and Rakim's "Don't Sweat the Technique"** from the album ***Don't Sweat the Technique*** (MCA, 1992). Eric B. and Rakim (also the producers of the track) looped the third bar of the "Give it Up" break as the beat for this song. They also enhanced some of George Brown's original kick drum sounds.

BREAKS

"Rocksteady"
Aretha Franklin
Young, Gifted, and Black (Atlantic, 1972)

This brings us back to the **"Rocksteady"** break. Notice **Bernard Purdie's** use of various three-16th-note patterns, beginning on the "and" of 2 in the third bar and continuing until the "and" of 2 in the fourth bar. This adds some tension to the break, which Purdie slickly resolves with that smooth open-hi-hat phrase.

♩ ≈105 bpm
▶ 2:29

Final Notes

The Thirteenth Element opens up a new realm of possibilities for breakbeats. Different combinations can also be played with 5-, 7-, or 9-note patterns. Don't forget that rests can also be included as part of the patterns. In addition, you can apply different sound sources, as well as other elements (especially buzz strokes, unisons, and open hi-hats) to the Thirteenth Element concepts.

THE ARCHITECTS ::

kool herc

Clive Campbell (a.k.a. Kool Herc) is often referred to as "the founding father of hip-hop." He was born on April 16, 1955 in Kingston, Jamaica. As a youth he was exposed to the sound systems and parties of the Kingston dance halls. He was also exposed to "toasting" (DJs talking over the tracks as they played). He moved with his family to the Bronx, NY, in 1967. Due to his height, and time spent lifting weights, his classmates gave him the nickname "Hercules." Herc began throwing parties in the rec room of his building at 1520 Sedgwick Ave. in the Bronx. This address is now officially recognized by New York State as "the birthplace of hip-hop." At these parties, Herc developed a DJ style that would eventually become the blueprint for hip-hop. He began playing the same drum break on two turntables, so when the break ended on one record, he would switch to the break on the other record. This process enabled him to keep the break going for as long as he wanted, and thus rock any party. He also began yelling various phrases through his mic, such as "to the beat y'all," and

"ya don't stop." This was the beginning of the art of rapping. In order to prevent other DJs from using the same records, Herc would soak the labels off of his so people couldn't see what he was spinning. He would spend hours digging through record crates, searching for the perfect drum breaks to rock his parties. He didn't care what the genre was, he was only concerned with the break. Herc's fame grew, and his parties became legendary events. For a time, Kool Herc was a folk hero in the Bronx. His popularity peaked in the mid-70s. Getting stabbed at one of his own parties led to the gradual waning of his fame. DJ Kool Herc spun his last old-school party in 1984. In 2007, Herc began a campaign to save 1520 Sedgwick Ave. from being sold to developers. As a result of his work, in 2008 the Deptartment of Housing Preservation and Development ruled against the sale of the building. Not only did Herc innovate an entire culture, he also saved his laboratory of creation from destruction. (www.oldschoolhiphop.com)

"Three-16th-Note" Phrase: **Exercises**

These exercises will help you get comfortable playing three-16th-note patterns over 4/4 time. They feature the patterns being played "over the bar line." This means the pattern is continuously repeated regardless of whether the measure has ended. Therefore, the three-16th-note pattern will appear at different places in each measure, until the pattern resolves itself. These patterns take three full measures to resolve (start back over on beat 1 of the measure). Count out loud when you practice these so you don't lose track of where you are in the measure. You can also move the right hand over to the ride, and play different patterns with your foot on the hi-hat. This will help you stay in time and also build coordination. Experiment with different accents and ghost notes as you practice these exercises. Remember to start slow and gradually increase the tempo.

Track 147

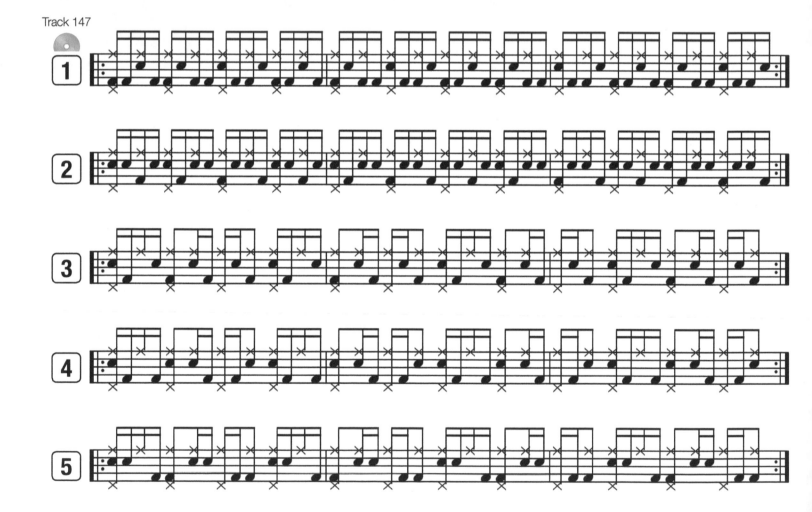

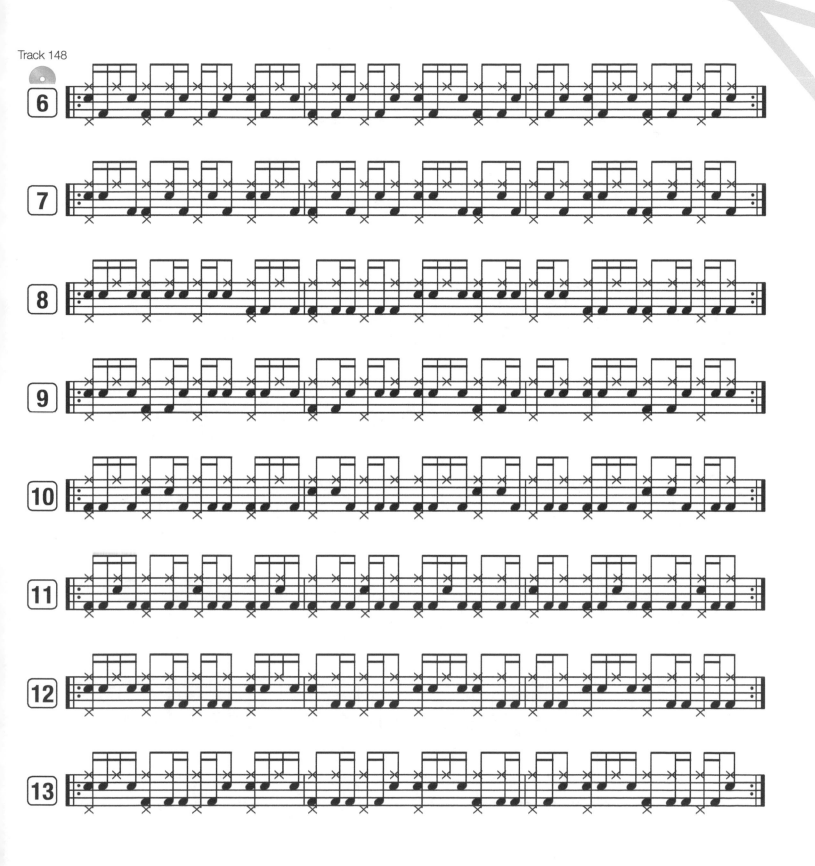

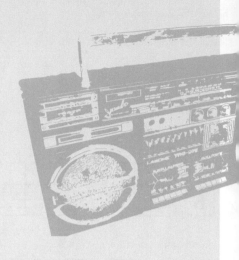

"Three-16th-Note" Phrase: **Beats**

This section contains two-bar beats featuring the Thirteenth
Element. As you practice these beats, focus on maintaining a steady
groove; don't let the pulse waver. Get comfortable with these beats
at a slow tempo (60 bpm) before you increase the speed. Remember,
snare notes without accents or ghost notes should be played mezzo
forte (medium loud).

Track 149

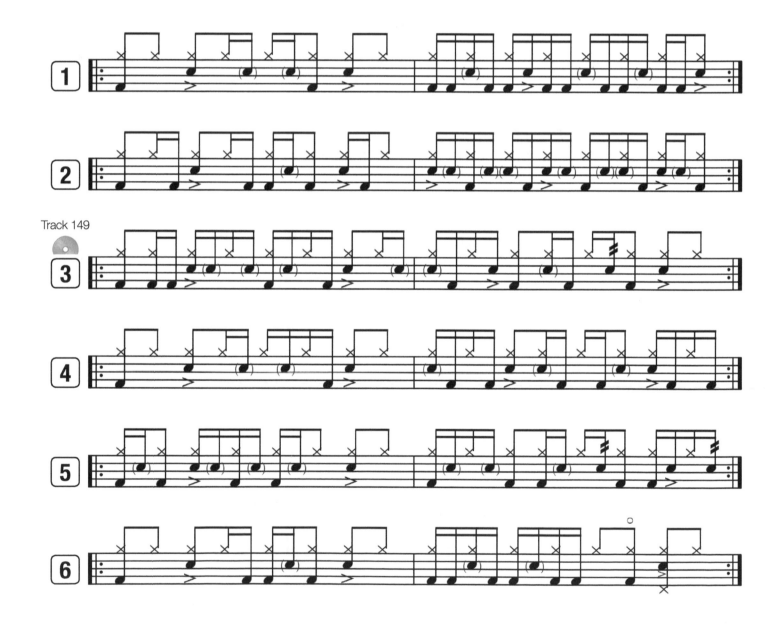

After you get comfortable with the Thirteenth Element beats, play the following two-bar beat before each of them:

This will turn each beat into a four-bar phrase. Play each new four-bar phrase 20 times, then move on to the next one.

"Three-16th-Note" Phrase: **8-Bar Phrase**

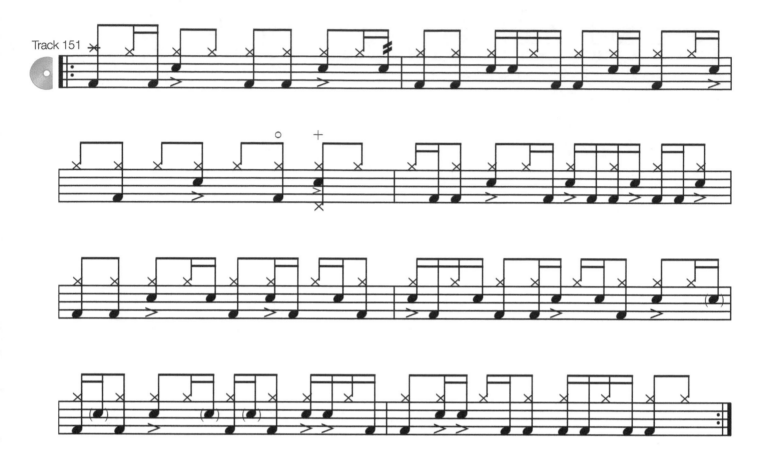

When you're comfortable with the eight-bar phrase, apply it to the following grid:

For the initial eight bars of groove, use any beat from the chapter, or make up your own.

Beats with Everything

This section features all of the elements mixed, matched, and applied to the beats. Have fun with these.

Track 152

After you're comfortable with the beats, play the following two-bar phrase before each of them:

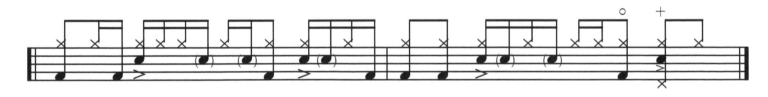

This will make each beat into a four-bar phrase. Practice each new four-bar phrase 20 times, then move on to the next one.

Beats with Everything: **8-Bar Phrase**

Track 155

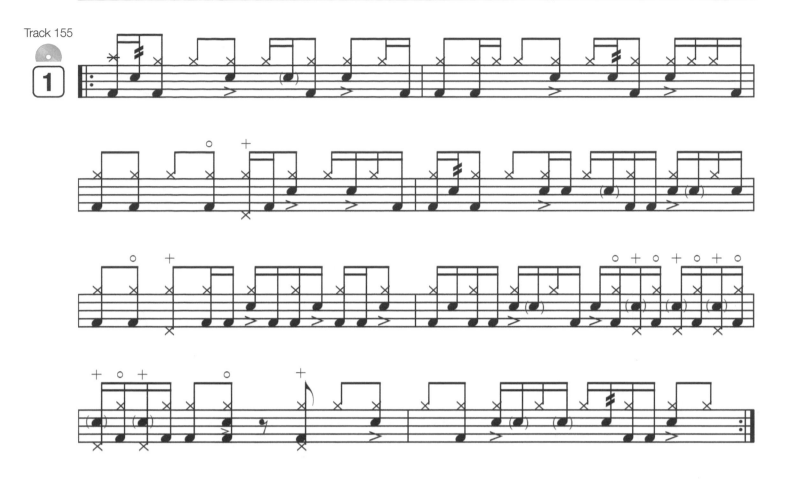

Beats with Everything: **8-Bar Phrase**

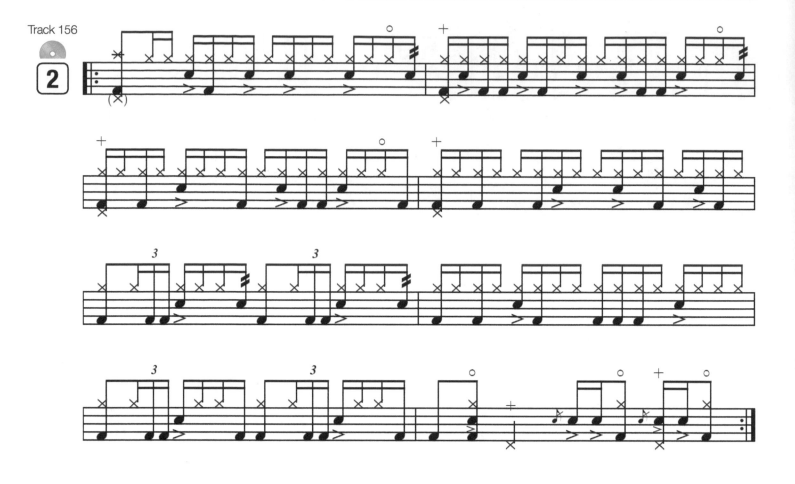

When you're comfortable with these phrases, apply them to the following grid:

Groove   8-Bar Phrase

For the initial eight bars of groove, use any beat from the book, or make up your own.

Beats with Drops

This chapter contains beats with full quarter note rests or more.

This serves multiple purposes. First, it will help you replicate the popular DJ/producer technique of cutting out the beat with the fader or kill switch, and then bringing it back in. Dropping out the beat brings attention to other aspects of the music, such as lyrics or samples. It also gives the beat added power when it's brought back in. This will add space and depth to your drumming. The technique can also be applied to the individual components of the drumset. For example, just the snare is cut out, or just the hi-hat is cut out.

Second, it will help strengthen your internal clock. Giving the drop it's full value without rushing or dragging the time might be difficult at first. That's because your playing has stopped. You have nothing to base the time on except for what's going on with your internal counting. If you have trouble with this, keep practicing with the click track while counting out loud. As you get these beats with drops tighter, your internal clock will be getting stronger. With enough practice, this chapter will enable you to utilize this technique in a live situation without rushing or dragging the time.

Here's a good example of a beat with drops. It's from the song **"Award Tour"** by **A Tribe Called Quest**, from the album ***Midnight Marauders*** (Jive/BMG Records, 1993). It features beat programming by the legendary **Ali Shaheed Muhammad**.

The song is based on this four-bar phrase:

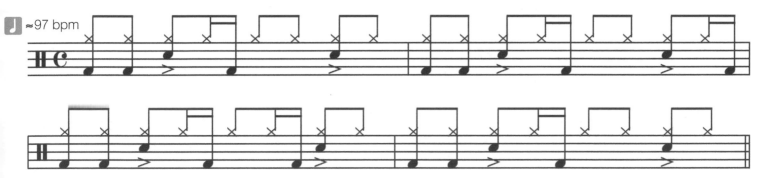

At 2:47, the beat is cut up like this:

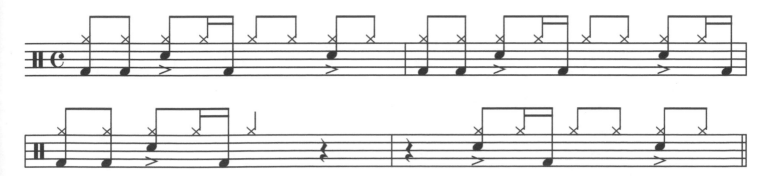

Notice how this creates space for the delay-drenched lyrics to come through. It also gives the beat added strength when it's brought back in.

Beats with Drops:

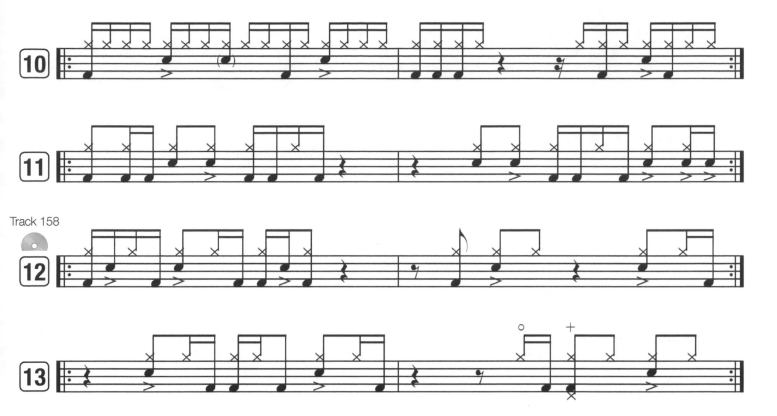

Track 158

When practicing this section, play each beat as written (as a two-bar phrase). As always, start slow (60 bpm) and gradually increase the tempo. Once you're comfortable with these, play the following two-bar phrase before each of them:

This will make each example into a four-bar phrase. Play each new four-bar phrase 20 times, then move on to the next one. This will give you a better understanding of how a beat with drops fits into a more musical context.

Fills

Fills are not an integral part of breakbeat drumming. However, they're still prevalent and can enhance your style when used sparsely. This section contains fill ideas that work well with breakbeats. Remember, the most important thing is the groove and the pocket. Fills are secondary and ornamental—but they're still fun as hell to play!

Track 160

Once you're comfortable with these fills, play the following two-bar phrase before each of them:

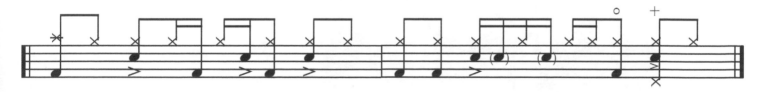

Play each new four-bar phrase 20 times, then move on to the next one.

"Scorpio"
Dennis Coffey and the Detroit Guitar Band
Evolution (Sussex, 1971)

This break features **Jack Ashford** on drums. The break starts at 1:10. Notice the fills in the second, fourth, and sixth bars. They're pretty simple, but they fit perfectly with the break. A lot of times, playing simply is the best thing you can do. It sounds as if the quarter note hi-hat part was over-dubbed, so just leave it out when you play the fills.

This break is most famously sampled on the **Young MC** song **"Bust a Move,"** off the album **Stone Cold Rhymin'** (Delicious Vinyl, 1988).

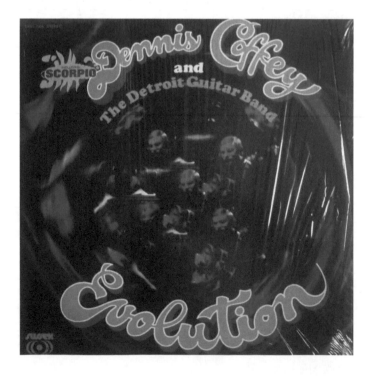

"Love the Life You Live"
Kool and the Gang
Music is the Message (De-Lite Records, 1972)

This break features the great **George Brown** on drums. Notice the fill in the eighth bar. It's a hand-foot-foot (three-16th-note) combo played around the toms. The break occurs at 2:37.

≈126 bpm

2:37

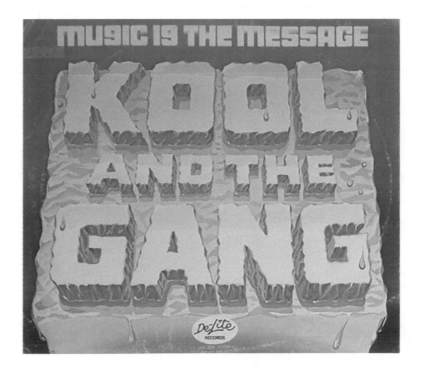

"Love the Life You Live"
Kool and the Gang
Music is the Message (De-Lite Records, 1972)

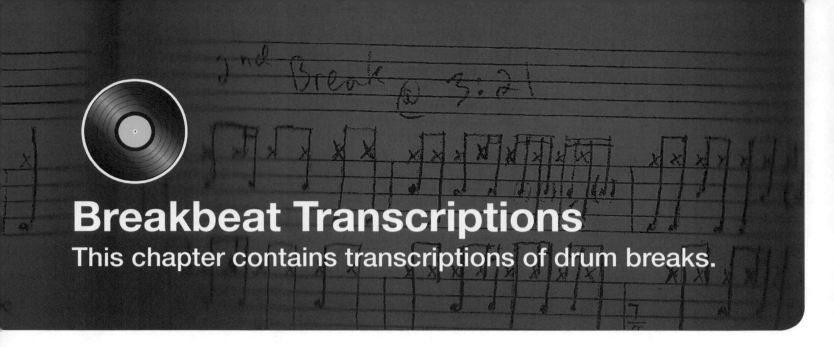

Breakbeat Transcriptions
This chapter contains transcriptions of drum breaks.

When studying these breaks, first listen to the entire song and get a feel for it. Transcriptions of the "main drum grooves" from the songs are included with some of these breaks. Compare and contrast these "main grooves" with the breaks. During drum breaks, the drummer will often increase the complexity and intensity of his/her beats. Listen for this to occur, and follow along with the transcriptions.

Where applicable, a few artists that have sampled these breaks are noted. Oftentimes, producers will sample the drum break, then reinforce it with processed kick and snare sounds. They'll also chop up the breaks and rearrange the pieces to make a new beat. In some cases, other parts of the song besides the drum break were sampled. This is also noted where applicable. Do some research to find out who else sampled these breaks, and for what. Obviously, all of the great drum breaks couldn't be included. The breaks in this section were selected based on their playability and interest for drummers, rather than the popularity of their usage as samples.

When you practice this section, learn the beats and breaks at a slower tempo (60 bpm). Gradually increase the speed. For some of the longer breaks, learn them bar by bar before you play the whole thing from start to finish. When you feel you're ready, practice them along with the recordings. Don't forget to record yourself and listen back.

This section is not necessarily meant to be studied from start to finish. Look through the entire chapter. Decide which breaks you're interested in learning first. Also, some of these breaks are more difficult to play than others. You might want to start out with some of the less challenging ones. In some instances, suggested stickings are included. Experiment with different stickings to find what works best for you.

This section also includes transcriptions of breakbeat drumming in context with other instruments and lyrics. This will help give you an understanding of how breakbeat drumming is applied to musical situations. (Note: The time markings for these breaks refer to their location in the original version of the song. These breaks are not included in *The Breakbeat Bible* audio.

The transcriptions are grouped into three different categories: **Classic Breaks**, **Deep Cuts**, and **Contemporary Beats**.

Classic Breaks

"God Made Me Funky"
The Headhunters

Survival of the Fittest (Arista, 1975)

Drums: Mike Clark

This track starts out with a timeless drum break featuring the Second Element (single 16th-note subdivisions on the kick), the Fifth Element (open hi-hat notes), and the Ninth Element (mixed hi-hat patterns). This is a very clean break. Notice the dry, controlled drum sound.

Here's the break at 0:00.

This break was sampled for **Eric B. and Rakim's "Beats for the Listeners,"** from the album ***Follow the Leader*** (UNI, 1988). It's a tight old-school jam from some of hip-hop's founding fathers.

"Funky Drummer
(Pts. 1 & 2)"

James Brown

released as a single (King Records, 1970)

In the Jungle Groove (Polydor, 1986)

Drums: Clyde Stubblefield

This funk masterpiece contains the "mother of all drum breaks." Clyde's performance is razor-sharp, and the drum sounds are immaculate. This makes it perfect for sampling. The break features the First Element (single 16th-note subdivisions on the snare), the Second Element (single 16th-note subdivisions on the kick), the Third Element (two 16th notes in a row on the snare), the Fifth Element (open hi-hat notes), the Seventh Element (buzz strokes on the snare), and the Eighth Element (steady 16th notes on the hi-hat with one hand). Clyde basically created the foundation of hip-hop with this break.

Here's the main drum groove from the beginning of the song (which Clyde slightly improvises on).

♩≈97 bpm

▶ 0:18

At 3:13, Clyde uses a beat similar to the first bar of the break at 5:22. He improvises off of this framework until the break hits. **Here's the break at 5:22.** Thousands of artists have sampled this break. There's also a notable break during the outro of the song, starting at 8:57.

♩≈101 bpm

▶ 5:22

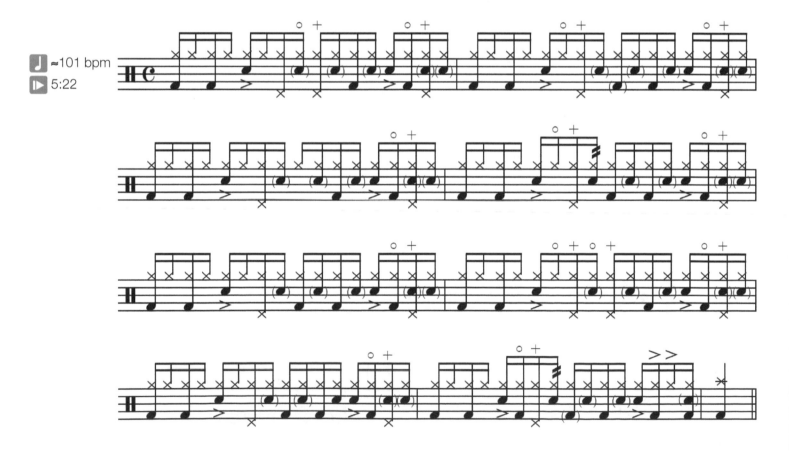

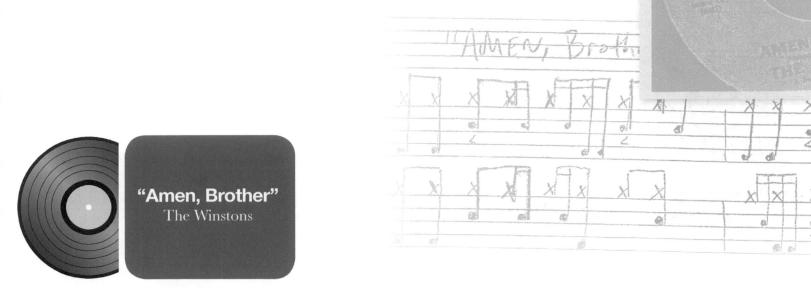

"Amen, Brother"
The Winstons

released as the B-side to the "Color Him Father" single (Metromedia Records, 1969)

Drums: Gregory C. Coleman

This up-tempo instrumental contains the "father of all drum breaks." It features the First Element (single 16th-note subdivisions on the snare), the Fourth Element (two 16th notes in a row on the kick), and the Sixth Element (syncopated accents on the snare). Notice the precise timing and the clean phrasing. Check out the tight, dry drum sounds. Although used extensively in hip-hop, this break is widely regarded as the foundation for Jungle, and later Drum'n'Bass.

Here's an interpretation of the main drum groove (which Coleman improvises on throughout the song).

♩ ≈129 bpm
▶ 0:17

Here's the break at 1:27. Thousands of artists have sampled this break.

♩ ≈137 bpm
▶ 1:27

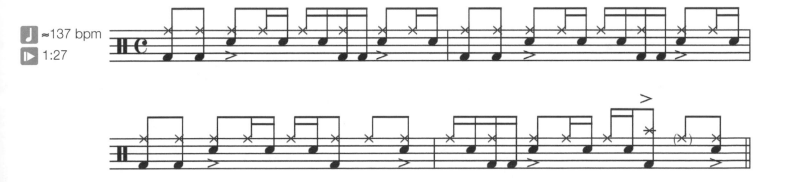

Directs and Dances with the James Brown Band- The Popcorn
(King Records, 1969)
Drums: Clyde Stubblefield

This is one of the most buttery drum breaks of all time. Weighing in at eighteen bars, this break features the First Element (single 16th-note subdivisions on the snare), the Third Element (plus pullouts into control stokes), the Sixth Element (syncopated accents on the snare), and the Seventh Element (buzz strokes on the snare). The drum sound is tight, but there's a little reverb on the snare which opens things up a bit. Clyde keeps it cool in the first four bars before exploding into pure breakbeat mastery.

Here's an interpretation of the main drum groove (which Clyde constantly improvises on throughout the song).

Here's the break at 3:16. Experiment with some different sticking options in order to pull this one off.

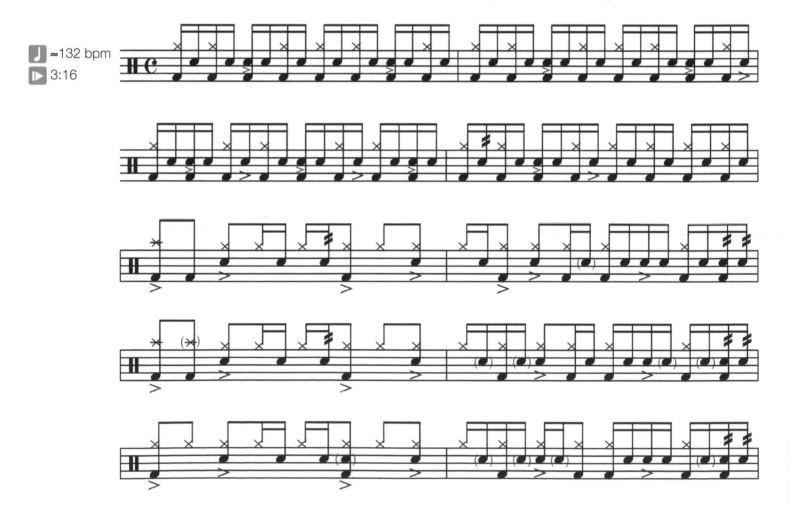

This break was sampled (and slowed down) for the **Digable Planet's** song **"9th Wonder (Blackitolism)"** from the album ***Blowout Comb*** (Pendulum Records, 1994). It sounds as if the ninth bar of Clyde's break is used as the first bar of the "9th Wonder" beat. It also sounds as if pieces of the sixth and twelfth bars of the "Soul Pride" break were used to create the second measure of the two-bar phrase that is the "9th Wonder" beat. Also, hand claps are added to the beat in the beginning of the song.

"Apache"
Michael Viner's
Incredible
Bongo Band

Bongo Rock (MGM Records, 1973)
Drums: Jim Gordon

This feel-good instrumental contains another classic drum break. It features the First Element (single 16th-note subdivisions on the snare). It's simple, but precise and clean. The drum sound is huge. This break occurs at the intro, but there are a few others throughout the song (including an extended one from 2:21 to 3:50). This is a rock-solid piece of hip-hop's foundation. "Apache" is sometimes known as "the Bronx national anthem."

Here's the break at 0:00. Thousands of artists have sampled this break. Also, check out the tight percussion patterns.

"Tighten Up"
Archie Bell and the Drells

Tighten Up (Atlantic, 1968)

Drums: Billy Butler

This is a classic funk track. The drum break occurs at 0:35, and features the First Element (single 16th-note subdivisions on the snare—and also a rack tom), and the Third Element (two 16th notes in a row on the snare). Also, check that fill at the end.

Here's the main drum groove (which is slightly improvised on throughout the song).

Here's the break at 0:35. Notice the switch from the hi-hat to the ride, as well as the busier snare pattern and added rack tom notes (a similar break also occurs at 1:55). It's easier to play those rack tom notes with the left hand. Also, it's difficult to hear if Butler is actually playing the ride cymbal on beats 2 and 4. Therefore, you can choose to play the snare on 2 and 4 with your right hand (and not play the ride on those beats).

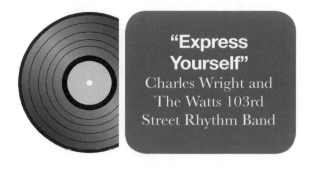

"Express Yourself"
Charles Wright and The Watts 103rd Street Rhythm Band

Express Yourself (Warner Bros. Records, 1970)
Drums: James Gadson

This is another classic. The break occurs at 1:39, in conjunction with a horn line. It features the First Element (single 16th-note subdivisions on the snare), the Second Element (single 16th-note subdivisions on the kick), the Third Element (two 16th notes in a row on the snare, including a pullout), the Fifth Element (very slightly open hi-hat notes), the Sixth Element (syncopated accents on the snare), the Seventh Element (buzz strokes on the snare), and the Eighth Element (steady 16th notes on the hi-hat with one hand). Gadson's drumming is silky smooth.

Here's the main drum groove of the song.

Here's the break at 1:39. Notice how Gadson incorporates the various elements while bending the beat to match/interact with the horn line. Also check out how the accented hi-hat notes add color to the beat.

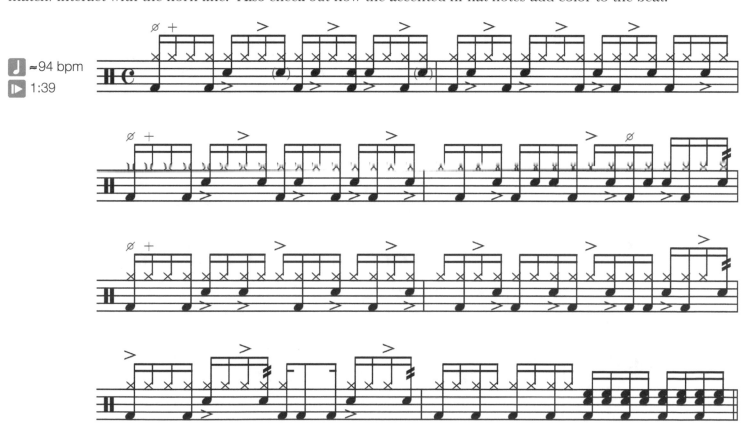

This song was sampled for **N.W.A's "Express Yourself,"** from the album ***Straight Outta Compton*** (Fourth and Broadway, 1988). Dr. Dre (the producer of the track) doubled the original kick, snare, and hi-hat sounds with enhanced sounds. He also used the original bass line, as well as various horn samples.

Still Bill (Sussex Records, 1972)

Drums: James Gadson

This is one of the greatest funk/soul songs of all time. The break occurs at 0:50, in conjunction with lyrics, and features the First Element (single 16th-note subdivisions on the rim click), the Second Element (single 16th-note subdivisions on the kick), the Fourth Element (two 16th notes in a row on the kick), the Fifth Element (open hi-hat notes), and the Eighth Element (steady 16th notes on the hi-hat with one hand). Another liquid break from Gadson. Check YouTube for live footage of Bill Withers performing this song with Gadson on drums.

Here's the main drum groove of the song.

Here's the break at 0:50 (similar breaks occur at 1:53 and 2:55).

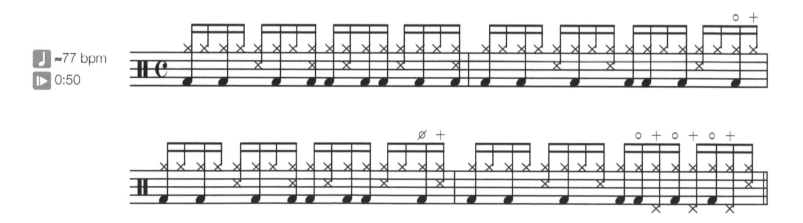

This song was sampled for the **UGK's "Use Me Up,"** from the album ***Too Hard to Swallow*** (Jive, 1992). Gadson's original kick, rim click, and hi-hat sounds from the main groove are doubled with enhanced sounds. Also, the guitar and clavinet line from the intro of Bill Withers' version were used for the UGK's beat.

Rhenium (HDH Records, 1990 reissue of *Osmium*, plus three singles)

Drums: either Ramon "Tiki" Fulwood or Tyrone Lampkin

This gritty offering starts with another classic drum break. It features the Fourth Element (two 16th notes in a row on the kick), the Fifth Element (open hi-hat notes), and the Ninth Element (mixed hi-hat patterns). Notice how the very subtle ghost notes on the hi-hat add texture to the beat. Check out the dirty drum sound drenched in reverb.

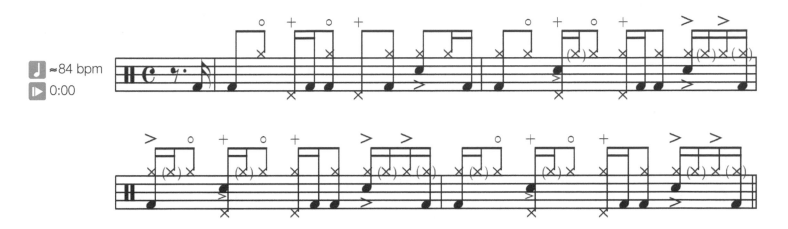

This break was sampled for **Company Flow's "Info Kill II,"** from the album ***Funcrusher Plus*** (Rawkus, 1997). El-P (the producer of the track) also used the bass line from "Come In Out of the Rain" for the "Info Kill II" beat.

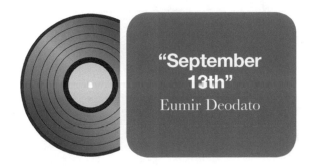

Prelude (CTI, 1972)

Drums: Billy Cobham

This smooth instrumental starts with a classic drum break. It features the First Element (single 16th-note subdivisions on the snare), the Second Element (single 16th-note subdivisions on the kick), and the Fifth Element (open hi-hat notes). Check out the reverb on the snare and the tight kick sound.

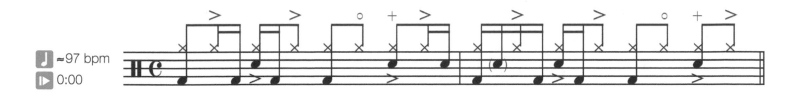

This song was sampled (and slightly slowed down) for the intro of **Pete Rock and C.L. Smooth's "In the House,"** from the album ***The Main Ingredient*** (Elektra, 1994). Pete Rock (the producer of the track) doubled the original kick drum sound with an enhanced kick drum sound. He also added a few extra kick drum notes. The original Rhodes and bass parts from "September 13th" were also used for the "In the House" intro beat.

"Here Comes the Meterman"
The Meters

The Meters (Josie Records, 1969)
Joseph "Zigaboo" Modeliste

This is a classic instrumental from the founding fathers of funk. The break occurs at 2:29. It features the First Element (single 16th-note subdivisions on the snare), The Second Element (single 16th-note subdivisions on the kick), the Third Element (two 16th notes in a row on the snare), the Fourth Element (two 16th notes in a row on the kick), the Fifth Element (an open hi-hat note), the Sixth Element (syncopated snare accents), the Twelfth Element (chordal drumming), and the Thirteenth Element (superimposing a three-16th-note phrase over 4/4). Check out the dirty, compressed drum sound.

Here's an interpretation of the main drum groove (which Zig constantly improvises on throughout the song). Notice how the right hand plays both the ride cymbal and the ride cymbal bell.

♩ ≈89 bpm

▶ 0:17

Here's the break at 2:29. Notice how Zig takes the framework of his groove for the song, changes it up, and mixes in the Twelfth and Thirteenth Elements. This is an approximation; there are a lot of little unaccountable sounds within the break, especially in the sixth and eighth bars. It's hard to tell exactly what's going on with the cymbal pattern in those bars (and perhaps there's also some foot splashes with the hi-hat?). Also, the notated cymbal crashes are more like accented ride notes (played with the shoulder of the stick). The cymbal bell sound is insane! Legend has it the sound was achieved with secret miking techniques. Listen for yourself and decide what's going on here.

This break was sampled for the **Digable Plantets** song **"Black Ego,"** from the album ***Blowout Comb*** (Pendulum Records, 1994). The first two measures of Zig's break were looped to make the beat for "Black Ego." Zig's original kick drum pattern is doubled with an enhanced kick drum sound, and two extra kick notes are added on the "ah" of 1 and the "e" of 2 in the first bar. There are also enhanced snare notes on beats 2, 4, and the "and" of 4 in the first bar, as well as beats 2 and 4 in the second bar (you can actually hear only the additional drum pattern at 3:52 in the song).

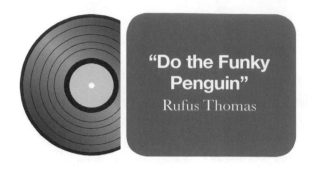

"Do the Funky Penguin"

Rufus Thomas

released as a single (Stax, 1971)

Drums: either Al Jackson Jr, Willie Hall, or Bobby Hunt

This is one of those old-school novelty dance songs, but the groove is nasty. The break occurs at the beginning of the song. It features the First Element (single 16th-note subdivisions on the snare), the Second Element (single 16th-note subdivisions on the kick), the Fourth Element (two 16th notes in a row on the kick), the Fifth Element (open hi-hat notes), and the Seventh Element (buzz strokes on the snare). Check out the tight, grainy, compressed drum sound. This is a fierce break, and it sets up the rest of the song perfectly.

Here's the break at 0:00.

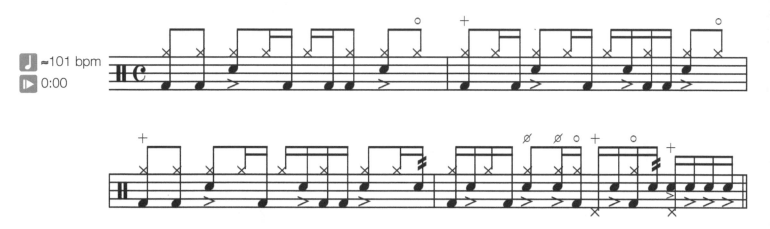

This break was sampled for **"The Grain"** by **Ghostface Killah featuring RZA**, from the album *Supreme Clientele* (Razor Sharp, 2000). RZA (the producer of the track) doubled the original kick drum pattern with an enhanced kick sound. He also added a few extra kick drum notes.

"I'm Glad
You're Mine"
Al Green

I'm Still In Love With You (Hi, 1972)
Drums: Al Jackson Jr.

This glassy soul track starts out with a classic drum break. The break features the First Element (single 16th-note subdivisions on the snare, here as rim clicks), the Second Element (single 16th-note subdivisions on the kick), the Third Element (two 16th notes in a row on the snare, here as rim clicks), and the Fifth Element (open hi-hat notes).

Here's the break at 0:00.

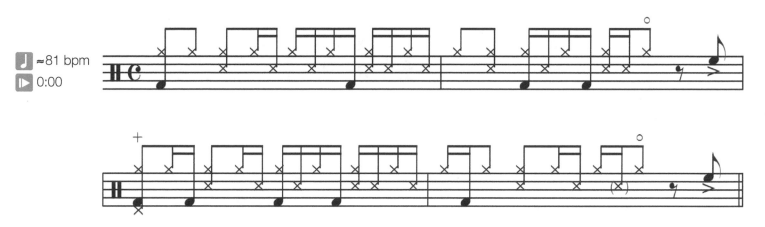

♩ ≈81 bpm
▶ 0:00

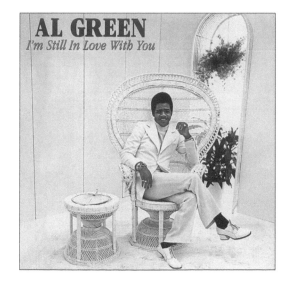

This break was sampled (and sped up) for **The Notorius B.I.G's "I Got A Story To Tell,"** from the album *Life After Death* (Bad Boy, 1997). Buck Wild (the producer of the track) chopped up and rearranged the first bar of the "I'm Glad You're Mine" break to make the beat for "I Got A Story To Tell." He also doubled some of the original kick drum notes with enhanced kick drum sounds, and added an extra note on the "and" of 1. This break was also sampled and chopped for **The Notorius B.I.G.'s "What's Beef?"** from *Life After Death*, and **"Dead Wrong,"** off his posthumous release *Born Again* (Bad Boy, 1999).

Deep Cuts

"The Crooked Cop"
The Bamboos

Step It Up (Ubiquity, 2006)
Drums: Danny Farrugia

Here's a slick instrumental from Australia's premier deep funk outfit. This break occurs at 0:53. It features the First Element (single 16th-note subdivisions on the snare), the Third Element [two 16th notes in a row on the snare (also check the pullout into the control stroke in the fourth measure)], the Fifth Element (open hi-hat notes), and the Seventh Element (buzz strokes on the snare). Check out the tight two bar fill at the end of the break. There's also a notable break at 2:13.

Here's an interpretation of the main groove.

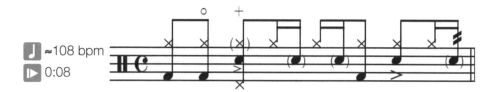

Here's the break at 0:53. Experiment to find the best sticking for yourself, especially during the last four bars of the break.

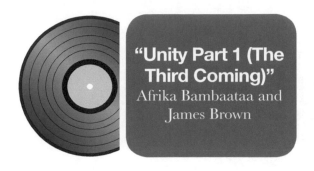

Unity (Tommy Boy Music, 1984)

Drums: Keith LeBlanc

This book had to include the collaboration between the "Godfather of Soul" and the "Godfather of Hip-Hop." It's a great old-school song with a positive message and a tight beat.

Here's the break at the start of the song. It features the First Element (single 16th-note subdivisions on the snare), and the Second Element (single 16th-note subdivisions on the kick).

Bambaataa raps over this four bar beat at 1:18. It features the First Element (single 16th-note subdivisions on the snare), the Second Element (single 16th-note subdivisions on the kick), the Fifth Element (an open hi-hat note), and the Ninth Element (mixed hi-hat patterns).

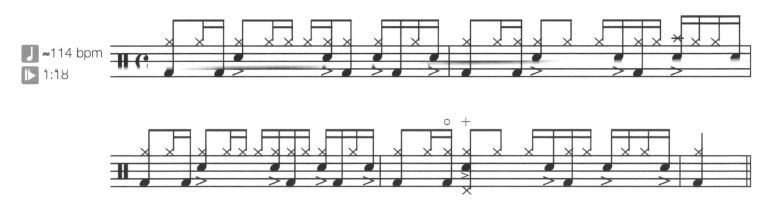

This two bar beat occurs at 1:26. It features the First Element (single 16th-note subdivisions on the snare), the Second Element (single 16th-note subdivisions on the kick), and the Third Element (two 16th notes in a row on the snare).

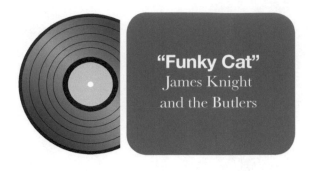

"Funky Cat"
James Knight
and the Butlers

Black Knight [CAT Records, 2008 (reissue)]
Drums: Robert "Blind" Jackson

This is a feel-good, underground, old-school funk track. The break occurs at 2:07, and features the First Element (single 16th-note subdivisions on the snare), the Second Element (single 16th-note subdivisions on the kick), the Third Element (two 16th notes in a row on the snare), the Fourth Element (two 16th notes in a row on the kick), the Fifth Element (open hi-hat notes), the Sixth Element (syncopated accents on the snare), the Seventh Element (buzz strokes on the snare), and the Thirteenth Element (a three-16th-note phrase superimposed over 4/4). Check out the heavy reverb on the snare for this kinetic drum break.

Here's the main drum groove of the song (which Jackson is constantly improvising on).

Here's the break at 2:07. Notice how Jackson switches to eighth notes on the hi-hat as the intensity of the kick and snare patterns increases in the sixth measure.

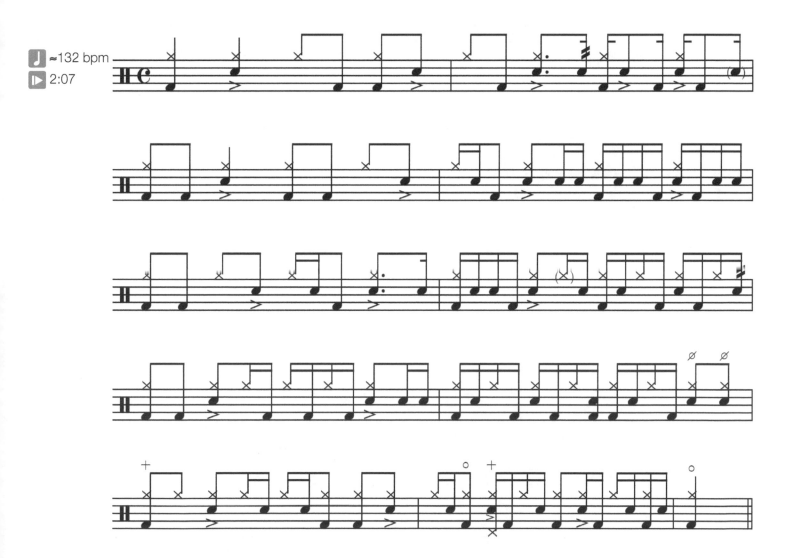

(Timco Records)

"Love At First Sight"
John Timmons

This tight instrumental starts with a nasty drum/bass groove. The drum pattern features the First Element (single 16th-note subdivisions on the snare), the Third Element (two 16th notes in a row on the snare, here as a control stroke), the Fourth Element (two 16th notes in a row on the kick), and the Ninth Element (mixed hi-hat patterns).

Here's the drum groove at the intro.

♩ ≈111 bpm
▶ 0:00

[released as a single (Rojac Records, 1969)]

"Baby Don't Cry"
The Third Guitar

This is gritty, old-school, deep funk. The song has two breaks. The first break features the First Element (single 16th-note subdivisions on the snare), the Second Element (single 16th-note subdivisions on the kick), the Third Element (two 16th notes in a row on the snare), the Fourth Element (two 16th notes in a row on the kick), the Sixth Element (syncopated accents on the snare), the Seventh Element (buzz strokes on the snare), and the Ninth Element (mixed hi-hat patterns, here on the ride cymbal). The second break features the same, plus the Thirteenth Element (superimposing a three-16th-note phrase over 4/4).

Here's the main groove of the song (which is constantly being improvised on).

♩ ≈96 bpm
▶ 0:01

Here's the first break at 1:09 (notice the switch from the hi-hat to the ride cymbal). This is just an approximation. It's difficult to hear exactly what's going on with the cymbal part, especially in measures five and six.

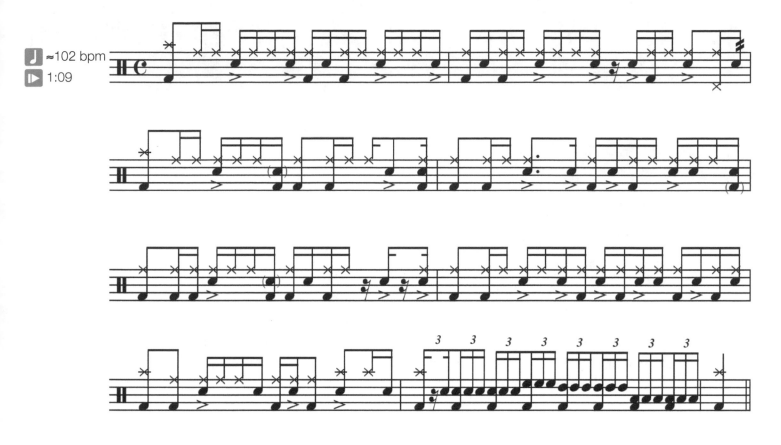

Here's the second break at 2:06 (again, notice the switch from the hi-hat to the ride cymbal).

Contemporary Beats

"Runnin"
The Pharcyde

Labcabincalifornia (Delicious Vinyl, 1995)
Drum Programming: Jay Dee a.k.a. J. Dilla

This is a classic track from one of the greatest hip-hop groups of all time. It features Jay Dee's unique drum programming. The kick pattern is constantly being improvised throughout the song. The beat is in the cracks between straight and swung. This is an eight-bar excerpt, which features the Second Element (single 16th-note subdivisions on the kick), the Fourth Element (two 16th notes in a row on the kick), and the Tenth Element (three 16th notes in a row on the kick). Check out the tight, dry drum sound. J. Dilla was a genius.

Here's an eight-bar phrase starting at 0:09.

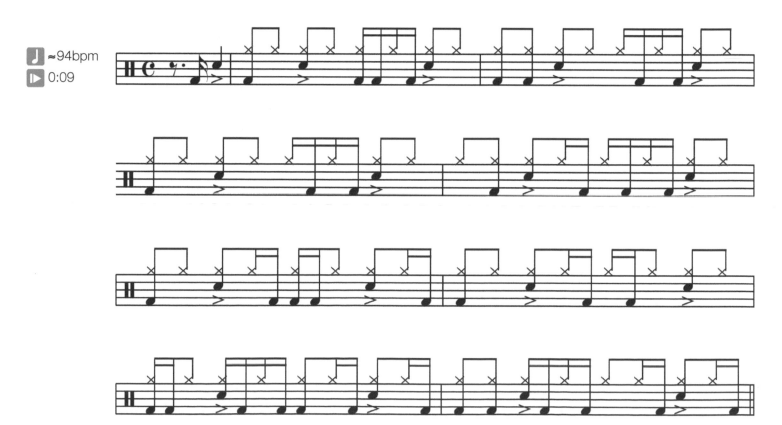

Hit The Floor (Ubiquity Records, 2005)
Drums: Miles Tackett

Besides drums, Miles also played guitar, bass, keyboards, and sang on this bouncy funk track. The drum pattern is slightly swung. The break occurs at 2:26, and features the First Element (single 16th-note subdivisions on the snare), the Second Element (single 16th-note subdivisions on the kick), the Third Element (two 16th notes in a row on the snare, here as control strokes), the Fourth Element (two 16th notes in a row on the kick), the Sixth Element (syncopated accents on the snare), and the Seventh Element (buzz strokes on the snare).

Here's an interpretation of the main drum groove (this four-bar phrase occurs at 0:25).

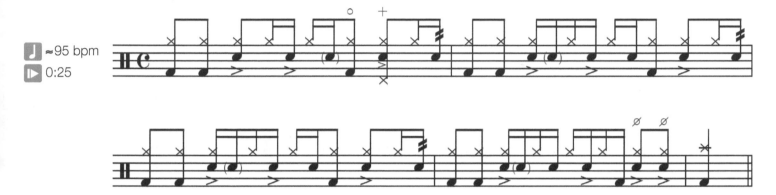

Here's the break at 2:26. Notice the switch from the hi-hat to the ride, as well as the increased syncopation. It sounds as if Tackett is playing the ride very close to the bell, but not quite on it. Also, the notated crashes in this transcription are more like accented ride cymbal notes (played with the shoulder of the stick).

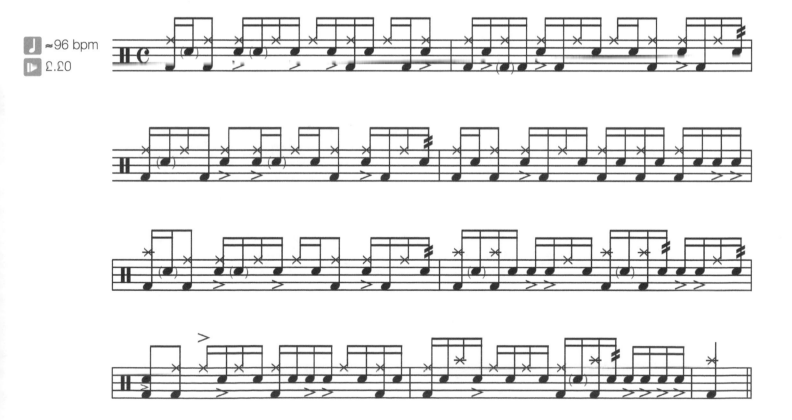

"Organ Donor"
DJ Shadow

Preemptive Strike (FFRR, 1997)
Production: DJ Shadow

This track features unique drum programming. Shadow programs like an improvising drummer; his patterns are constantly shifting throughout the song.

Here's the four-bar phrase at 0:09. It features the First Element (single 16th-note subdivisions on the snare), and the Fourth Element (two 16th notes in a row on the kick).

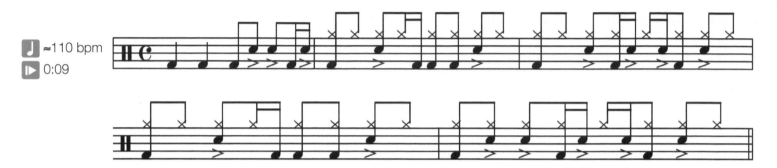

Here's a two-bar phrase at 0:59. It features the Second Element (single 16th-note subdivisions on the kick), the Third Element (two 16th notes in a row on the snare), and the Fourth Element (two 16th notes in a row on the kick).

Here's a four-bar phrase at 3:25. It features the First Element (single 16th-note subdivisions on the snare, the Second Element (single 16th-note subdivisions on the kick), the Third Element (two 16th notes in a row on the snare), the Fourth Element (two 16th notes in a row on the kick), and the Sixth Element (syncopated accents on the snare).

Here's an eight-bar phrase at 3:34. It features the First Element (single 16th-note subdivisions on the snare), the Second Element (single 16th-note subdivisions on the kick), the Third Element (two 16th notes in a row on the snare), the Fourth Element (two 16th notes in a row on the kick), and the Sixth Element (syncopated accents on the snare).

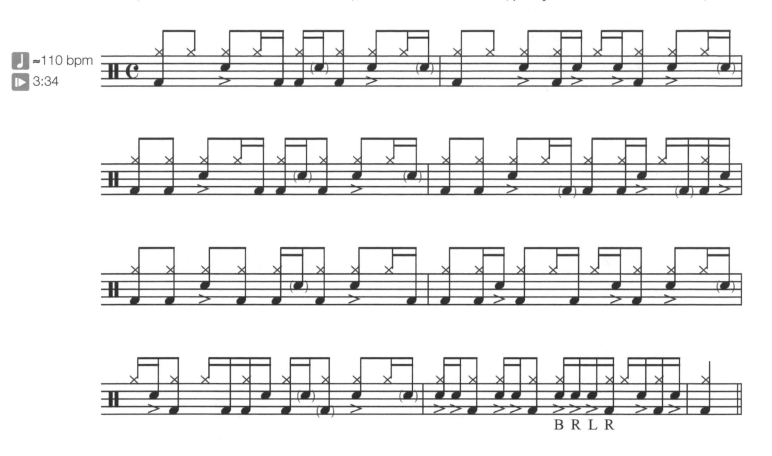

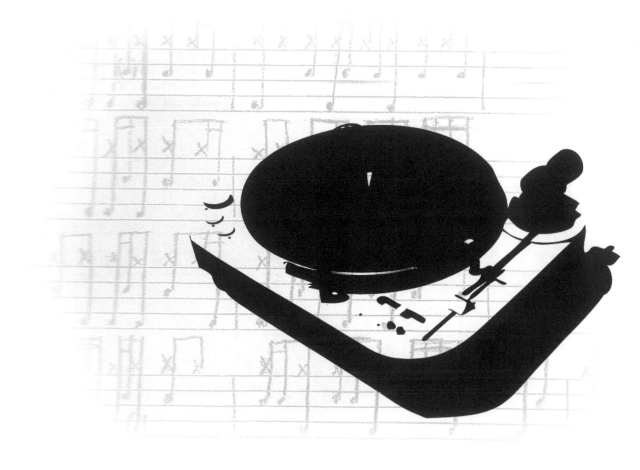

"Ain't It Hard"
Sharon Jones
and the Dap Kings

Dap Dippin' With...
(Daptone Records, 2002)
Drums: Homer Steinweiss

These guys are the kings of the funk and soul revivalist movement. This is a driving funk track with three tight drum breaks. Check out the dry snare sound paired with a resonant kick drum sound.

Here's an interpretation of the main groove from the verses (Homer is constantly improvising on this throughout the song).

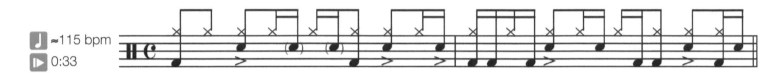

This break occurs at 0:00. It features the First Element (single 16th-note subdivisions on the snare), the Third Element (two 16th notes in a row on the snare), and the Sixth Element (a syncopated accent on the snare).

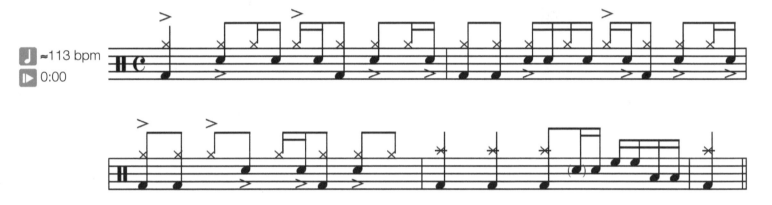

This break at 1:32 was discussed in the Third Element chapter of the book (pg. 27).

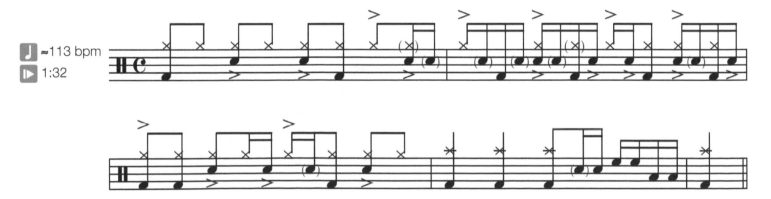

Here's the break at 3:21. It features the First Element (single 16th-note subdivisions on the snare), and the Sixth Element (syncopated accents on the snare). This break contains some interesting phrasing, notated here with a measure of 9/8 and a measure of 7/8. It's easier to count and feel it like that, as opposed to displacing everything by an eighth note in bars 5, 6, and 7.

♩ ≈115 bpm
▶ 3:21

"Speak E.Z."
Lettuce

Rage! (Velour Recordings, 2008)
Drums: Adam Deitch

This nasty instrumental track features ultra-tight drumming in the vein of Zigaboo Modeliste. Deitch is featured on five separate two-bar breaks which collectively contain the First Element (single 16th-note subdivisions on the snare), the Second Element (single 16th-note subdivisions on the kick), the Third Element (two 16th notes in a row on the snare), the Fourth Element (two 16th notes in a row on the kick), the Fifth Element (open hi-hat notes), the Sixth Element (syncopated accents on the snare), the Seventh Element (buzz strokes on the snare), the Ninth Element (mixed hi-hat patterns), the Twelfth Element (chordal drumming), and the Thirteenth Element (superimposing a three-16th-note phrase over 4/4). Deitch draws from an extensive wellspring of licks and ideas for this track. Check out the bright, poppy, open snare sound, and tight kick sound.

Here's the four-bar phrase that Deitch plays at 0:00.

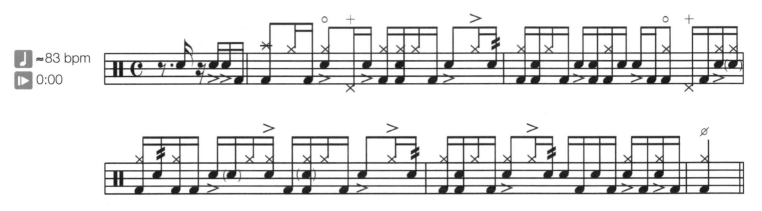

His drum pattern not only matches the rest of the band, but it also interacts with what they're doing. He improvises off of this framework throughout the song, especially during the breaks.

Here's the break at 0:47.

Here's the break at 1:16.

Here's the break at 1:56.

Here's the break at 2:24.

Here's the break at 3:15.

"...And I'm Out"
Galactic
featuring Mr. Lif

From the Corner to the Block (Anti-, 2007)
Drums: Stanton Moore

This album finds Galactic collaborating with various hip-hop artists (a marked departure from other Galactic albums). The song is built on a grinding beat from Stanton, which features the First Element (single 16th-note subdivisions on the snare), the Second Element (single 16th-note subdivisions on the kick), and the Ninth Element (mixed hi-hat patterns). The groove doesn't quite do justice to the vast wealth of Stanton's skills; it's included because of the band/MC collaboration factor. The drumming is toned down to accommodate the lyrics; this is a great example of playing for the song as opposed to unleashing raw chops. Basically, though, check out anything Stanton has ever done to hear his mastery of the instrument.

Here's an interpretation of the main drum groove. This pattern slightly morphs throughout the song.

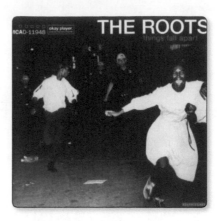

Things Fall Apart (MCA Records, 1999)

Drums: Ahmir "Questlove" Thompson

This was The Roots' most mainstream song at the time (aimed at the "unconscious masses"). However, Questlove was still able to sneak in this tight Drum'n'Bass passage during the song's outro. This is cool because it's a live drummer replicating the beats of producers who were speeding up samples of live drummers playing beats. It's the full circle, and Questlove's tight, clean performance here demonstrates his Jedi mastery. Notice the controlled, compressed drum sound.

Here's the main drum groove at 0:00.

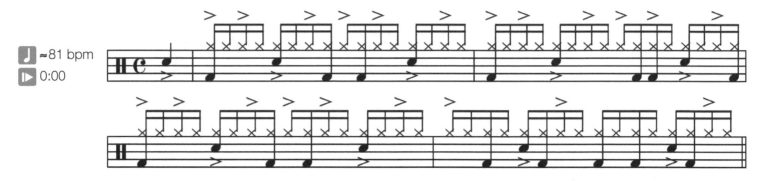

Here's the Drum 'n' Bass passage at 3:30. The tempo is 81 bpm with an implied double-time feel of 162 bpm.

Fade Out

"You Know I'm No Good"

Amy Winehouse

Back to Black (Universal Island Records, 2006)

Drums: Homer Steinweiss

This is a great song from the U.K.'s most popular soul revivalist. The song starts with a tight drum break reminiscent of the "Impeach the President" break. It features the First Element (single 16th-note subdivisions on the snare), the Third Element (two 16th notes in a row on the snare), the Fifth Element (open hi-hat notes), and the Seventh Element (buzz strokes on the snare). There's another drum break at 1:10 that features the same elements as the first break (minus the Seventh Element).

Here's the break at 0:00.

≈104 bpm

0:00

Here's the break at 1:10.

≈102 bpm

1:10

Click Track Loops
Use a drum machine to program these loops.

You should be comfortable playing the exercises and beats of this book with a standard quarter note click track before playing them with any of the Click Track Loops. You don't necessarily have to finish the other sections of the book with a standard click before moving onto the Click Track Loops. You can use the loops while you're working through the book as long as you're comfortable with the quarter note click.

It's highly beneficial to practice the beats, exercises, and transcriptions from the book to these loops. It will greatly improve your timing, smooth out and tighten up your beats, and strengthen your internal clock. Different loops will have different benefits. These will be discussed as the loop is presented. Practice all of the exercises and beats from the book with the Click Track Loops. When doing this, really analyze the exercise or beat you're working on before you play it. Figure out what parts of the exercise or beat line up with the Click Track Loop you're working with. This will help you lock in with the loop. Once you have an exercise or beat locked in with a loop, hold it for five minutes before moving on to the next one.

Non-traditional Metronome Usage

If you don't have a drum machine you can still use a regular metronome in non-traditional ways. For example, if you're practicing something at 90 bpm, you can set the metronome to 45 bpm. This way, you're using your internal clock to generate every other beat. You can also shift the way you're hearing the click. Instead of having the click be the downbeats, make yourself hear it as the "e," "and," or "ah" of the beat. To do this, start counting time 1, 2, 3, 4, 1, 2, 3, 4, etc. before you start the metronome. Then start the metronome on the "e," "and," or "ah" of the beat. See if you can tap out quarter notes with your foot and count out loud while holding the click on this other partial. Get comfortable with that before you start playing the beats and exercises with these non-traditional metronome techniques.

Click Track Loop #1:

One-bar loop with the click on the 2 and 4.

This will help you use your internal clock to generate the 1 and 3 of the beat.

Here's the loop:

Work to line up whatever you're playing on beats 2 and 4 with the clicks from the loop. For example, in this basic beat, the snare is playing on beats 2 and 4. Notice how the snare lines up with the click from the loop:

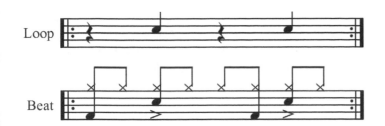

Get comfortable playing this basic beat to the click track loop. Then, use the loop to practice the other exercises and beats from the book.

Now, let's take Exercise #1 from the First Element chapter of the book. This is how the exercise lines up with this click track loop:

Notice how there's a kick drum and a hi-hat on beats 2 and 4 of the exercise. Work to line these up with the clicks from the loop. Once you're comfortable with this, move on to the rest of the exercises in the book. To gain the full benefit of this process, play each exercise for five minutes before moving on to the next one. It's important to begin slow, and gradually speed up the tempo of the loops.

Now let's take Beat #1 from the First Element chapter. This is how the beat lines up with the click track loop:

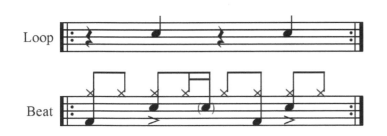

Notice both the snare and hi-hat playing on beats 2 and 4 of the measure. Again, work to make sure these are lined up with the click from the loop. Once you're comfortable with this, move on to the rest of the beats from the book. To gain the full benefit of this process, play each beat for five minutes before moving on to the next one. Start slow and gradually speed up the tempo of the loops.

Once you're comfortable with this one-bar loop, you can make it into a two-bar loop. The first measure is the same as above, and the second measure is a four beat rest. Here's the loop:

Practicing to this loop will further develop the internal clock, because you'll be forced to generate the four beats of the second measure of the loop.

Hint: Start the loop and let it repeat a few times. Get comfortable just tapping out quarter notes with your foot and counting time out loud. It may be difficult at first to stay in time as the second measure of the loop passes in silence. If the click on beat 2 of the first measure happens before you think it should, it means you slowed down during the second measure. Likewise, if the click on beat 2 of the first measure happens after you think it should, it means that you sped up during the second measure of the loop. Keep at it until you can match the loop through the silence and land on beat 2 of the first measure right in time.

Let's take the same basic beat and play it with this loop. This is how two measures of the beat line up with the loop:

Once you're comfortable playing this basic beat with the loop, move on to the rest of the beats and exercises in the book.

Here's what Exercise #1 from the First Element chapter looks like when lined up with the loop:

Here's what Beat #1 from the First Element chapter looks like when lined up with the loop:

As you get more comfortable with this, you can begin adding more measures of silence. Here's a four-bar loop with the click on 2 and 4 of the first bar; the last three measures are silent:

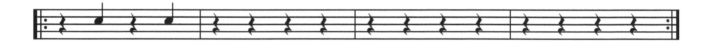

You can apply this concept of adding on measures of silence to the rest of the Click Track Loops.

Click Track Loop #2

One-bar loop with the click on the "and" of every beat.

This will help strengthen your internal clock, because you'll have to stay rock steady in order to prevent the click from drifting back to the downbeats. Here's the loop:

Start by just tapping out quarter notes (with your foot, on the floor) and counting out loud as the loop plays:

Let's take the same basic beat and play it with this loop. This is how the beat lines up with the loop:

Notice how there are hi-hat notes on the "and" of every beat of the measure. Use these to help you lock in with the loop.

Here's what Exercise #1 from the First Element chapter looks like when lined up with the loop:

Notice the hi-hat notes on the "and" of every beat. Focus on this to help you lock in with the loop.

Here's what Beat #1 from the First Element chapter looks like when lined up with the loop:

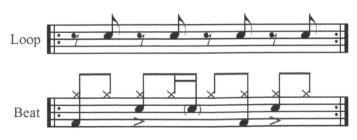

Again, notice the hi-hat notes on the "and" of every beat. Use these to help you lock in with the loop.

Click Track Loop #3

One-bar loop with the click on the "e" of every beat.

This will help strengthen your internal clock because you'll have to play rock steady in order to prevent the click from drifting from the "e's" back to the downbeats. This loop also helps smooth out and tighten up your beats because you have to place all of the kick, snare, and hi-hat notes very precisely in order to fit them with the "on-the-e" click track. Here's the loop:

Start by just tapping out quarter notes with your foot and counting out loud as the loop plays:

The slower the tempo of the loop, the easier it will be to make this happen. Start at 60 bpm, and don't increase the tempo until you're comfortable.

Once you're comfortable with this, play the same basic beat with the loop. This is what the beat looks like when lined up with the loop:

Notice how there is nothing playing on the "e" during any of the beats of the measure. Allow the click to fall in between the hi-hat notes, and hold steady. If you waiver at all, you'll be able to tell immediately. Keep at it until your beat is smoothed out and tight, and you can maintain the click on the "e's."

This is what Exercise #1 from the First Element chapter looks like when lined up with the loop:

Notice the snare playing on the "e" of every beat. Focus to match up your snare part with the clicks on the "e's."

This is what Beat #1 from the First Element chapter looks like when lined up with the loop:

Loop

Beat

Notice that there's nothing playing on the "e" during any beat of the measure. Allow the click to fall in between the other notes, and keep it tight.

Click Track Loop #4

One-bar loop with the click on the "ah" of every beat.

Like Click Track Loop #3, this will also help strengthen the internal clock. You'll have to stay rock steady in order to prevent the click from drifting from the "ah's" back to the downbeats. This loop also helps smooth out and tighten up your beats because you have to place all of the kick, snare, and hi-hat notes with precision in order to fit them with the "on-the-ah" click track. Here's the loop:

Start by tapping out quarter notes with your foot and counting out loud:

Loop

Again, the slower the tempo of the loop, the easier it will be to make this happen. Start at 60 bpm and gradually increase the tempo.

Foot
(on floor)
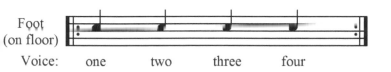
Voice: one   two   three   four

When you get comfortable with this, play the same basic beat with the loop. This is what the beat looks like when lined up with the loop:

Loop

Beat

Notice there is nothing playing on the "ah" of the beat. In order to lock this beat in with the loop, let the click fall on the "ah's" in between the hats, and keep your kick, snare, and hi-hat parts tight.

This is what Exercise #1 from the First Element chapter looks like when lined up with this loop:

Notice there is nothing playing on the "ah" during any beat of the measure. Let the click fall on the "ah's" and play everything else around it.

This is what Beat #1 from the First Element chapter looks like when lined up with the loop:

Notice the snare note on the "ah" of 2. Focus on lining that note up with the "ah" of 2 from the click track. Let everything else fall around the rest of the clicks, and keep it smooth and tight.

Click Track Loop #5

One-bar loop with the click on the "e" of 1 and the "e" of 3.

This will help strengthen the internal clock because you'll have to generate the second and fourth beat on your own. It will also help smooth out and tighten up your beats because you'll have to lock in with the "e's" of 1 and 3. In addition, it'll help you dial in the downbeats: If you're too slow on the downbeat, you'll flam with the click track. If you're rushing the downbeat, there will be too much space between your downbeat and the click. This will give you the control to be able to play straight down the middle. It'll also give you the control to be able to place the downbeats ahead of the beat or behind the beat as the musical situation requires. Here's the loop:

Start by tapping out quarter notes with your foot and counting out loud along with the loop:

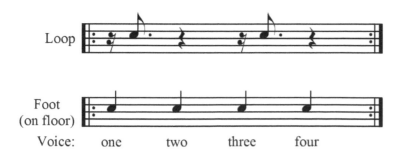

The slower the tempo of the loop, the easier it will be to make this happen. Start at 60 bpm and gradually increase the tempo.

This is what the basic beat looks like when matched up with the loop:

This is what Exercise #1 from the First Element chapter looks like when matched up with the loop:

This is what Beat #1 from the First Element chapter looks like when matched up with the loop:

Click Track Loop #6

One-bar loop with the click on the "ah" of 2 and the "ah" of 4.

This will help strengthen the internal clock, smooth out and tighten up your beats, and improve your timing. Also, as with Click Track Loop #5, this will help you dial in the downbeats. This time, if you're rushing the downbeats, you'll flam with the click because the click is anticipating the downbeats. If you're lagging on the downbeats, there will be too much time between the click and your downbeat. Here's the loop:

Again, don't forget to start slow.

Begin by tapping out quarter notes with your foot and counting out loud along with the loop:

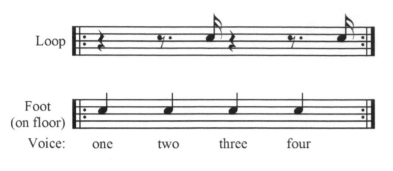

Loop

Foot (on floor)

Voice: one   two   three   four

This is what the basic beat looks like when matched up with the loop:

Loop

Beat

This is what Exercise #1 from the First Element chapter looks like when matched up with the loop:

Loop

Exercise

This is what Beat #1 from the First Element chapter looks like when matched up with the loop:

Loop

Beat

Click Track Loop #7

One-bar loop with the click on the "e" of 2 and the "e" of 4.

This will help strengthen the internal clock, smooth out and tighten up your beats, and improve your timing. This loop will also help you dial in your backbeats (snare on 2 and 4). In order to lock in with the loop you'll have to precisely place the snare on beats 2 and 4. If you're too slow, you'll flam with the click, and if you're too fast, there will be too much time between your snare note and the click. After some work with this, you'll be able to lay it right down the middle. You'll also develop the control to be able to play behind the beat or ahead of the beat, if the music calls for it. Here's the loop:

Remember to start slow.

Again, start by tapping out quarter notes with your foot and counting out loud along with the loop:

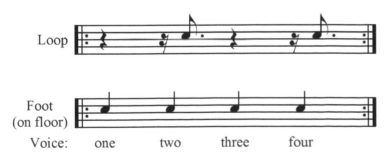

Loop

Foot (on floor)

Voice: one   two   three   four

This is what the basic beat looks like when matched up with the loop:

This is what Exercise #1 from the First Element chapter looks like when matched up with the loop:

This is what Beat #1 from the First Element chapter looks like when matched up with the loop:

Click Track Loop #8

One-bar loop with the click on the "ah" of 1 and the "ah" of 3.

This will help strengthen your internal clock, smooth out and tighten up your beats, and improve your timing. Like Click Track Loop #7, this will help you dial in your backbeats as well. If your backbeat is too fast, you'll flam with the click because the click is anticipating the backbeat. If it's too slow, there will be too much time between the click and your backbeat. This will help you get comfortable with playing behind or ahead of the beat, if the music calls for it. It will also help you realize what it feels like to lay it right down the middle. Here's the loop:

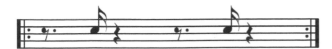

Start by tapping out quarter notes with your foot and counting out loud along with the loop:

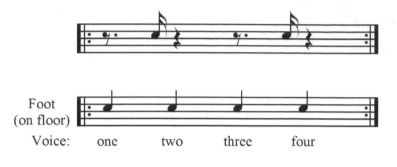

Foot (on floor)

Voice: one two three four

This is what Exercise #1 from the First Element chapter looks like when matched up with the loop:

Loop

Exercise

This is what the basic beat looks like when matched up with the loop:

Loop

Beat

This is what Beat #1 from the First Element chapter looks like when matched up with the loop:

Loop

Beat

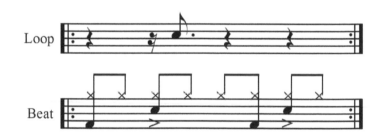

Other Ideas

1️⃣ Program a one measure loop, with just one note. Make this note anything, such as (in this case) the "ah" of 1:

Or here, the "e" of 2:

Loop

Beat

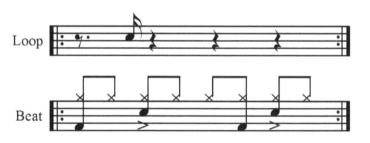

2️⃣ Program a two-measure loop, with just one note. Make this note anything, such as (in this case) the "e" of 3:

Loop

Beat

Or here, the "ah" of 3:

Loop

Beat

[3] Use Click Track Loop #1, and make it into a two-measure loop by adding a measure of silence. However, instead of playing continuously over the loop, you rest when the loop is silent. Here's what this concept looks like with the basic beat:

Loop

Beat

This will really help your internal clock, because you'll be forced to keep time without playing anything.

[4] Use Click Track Loop #1, and make it into a four-measure loop by adding 3 measures of silence. Then, play a measure of beat, rest for a measure, play a measure of beat, and rest for another measure. Here's what that concept looks like with Beat #1 from the First Element chapter:

Loop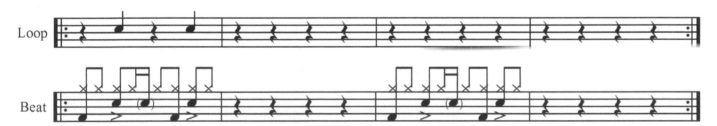

Beat

This will also help your internal clock because you'll be alternating between resting for a measure and playing for a measure. You'll have to count steady through resting and playing while doing this, since there are three bars of silence in the loop.

[5] Instead of using Click Track Loop #1 for ideas #3 and #4, use any of the Click Track Loops.

[6] Program a one measure loop with just one click note on beat 1. This loop is not quite as challenging as some of the others. However, it's still very effective in strengthening the internal clock and tightening up your groove.

[7] Make up your own Click Track Loops.

[8] Have fun being a drum geek.

Dubstep

Dubstep music is characterized by heavy, oscillating, synthesized bass patterns layered with other instruments, samples, effects, and (sometimes) vocals. This genre can either be felt in cut time (about 130-150 bpm), or half time (about 65-75 bpm). The drums of the Dubstep style are programmed, but can be reproduced on an acoustic drumset. The snare plays on the 2 and 4 (or on beat 3 in cut time). (Note: Technically, in some circles, if there are any other snare notes besides 2 and 4, or beat 3 in cut time, it's not a Dubstep beat. However, this section features beats with extra snare notes to make them applicable to other contemporary genres such as Glitch-Hop, Trip-Hop, and Downtempo.) The kick plays minimal but syncopated patterns around the snare. The hi-hats primarily play 16th notes, sometimes broken up, sometimes interspersed with 32nd-note subdivisions. The beats of this genre sometimes have implied 8th-note triplets on the kick and/or snare, which is featured in some of the examples in this section. This is a popular contemporary genre. The concept of DJs combining forces with live drummers is beginning to gain momentum, so it would be a good idea to get comfortable with this style of beats. (Note: Use alternating sticking for the 32nd-note hi-hat patterns. Check out beat #8.)

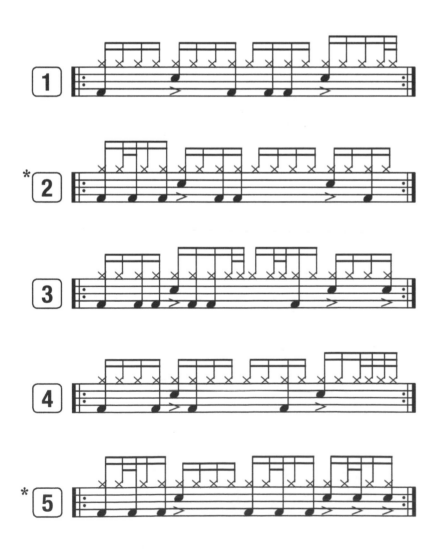

RLRLR R   RLR RLR R

Track 161

Track 162

*These beats feature implied triplets on the kick and/or snare.

Here's the drum pattern for the song **"Custard Chucker,"** by **Caspa and Rusko**. This is an interpretation of what the kick, snare, and hi-hat would play on an acoustic drumset. There are a lot of electronic sounds that add to the beat, but this is the basic drum pattern.

Breakography

Archie Bell and the Drells
Tighten Up (Atlantic, 1968)
Drums: Billy Butler

Charles Wright and The Watts 103rd Street Rhythm Band
Express Yourself (Warner Bros. Records, 1970)
Drums: James Gadson

Bill Withers
Still Bill (Sussex Records, 1972)
Drums: James Gadson

Eumir Deodato
Prelude (CTI, 1972)
Drums: Billy Cobham

Parliament
Rhenium (HDH Records, 1990 reissue of *Osmium*, plus three singles)
Drums: Ramon "Tiki" Fulwood, Tyrone Lampkin

The Meters
The Meters (Josie Records, 1969)
Drums: Zigaboo Modeliste

Al Green
I'm Still In Love With You (Hi, 1972)
Drums: Al Jackson Jr., Howard Grimes

The Headhunters
Survival of the Fittest (Arista, 1975)
Drums: Mike Clark

James Knight and the Butlers
Black Knight [CAT Records, 2008 (reissue)]
Drums: Robert "Blind" Jackson

Michael Viner's Incredible Bongo Band
Bongo Rock (MGM Records, 1973)
Drums: Jim Gordon

Carleen and the Groovers
Can We Rap [Now-Again Records, 2004 (reissue)]
Drums: Carleen Jean Butler

Afrika Bambaata and James Brown
Unity (Tommy Boy Music, 1984)
Drums: Keith LeBlanc

DJ Shadow
Preemptive Strike (FFRR, 1998)
Production: DJ Shadow

Amy Winehouse
Back to Black (Universal Island Records, 2006)
Drums: Homer Steinweiss, Troy Auxilly-Wilson, Salaam Remi

Sharon Jones and the Dap Kings
Dap Dippin' With... (Daptone Records, 2002)
Drums: Homer Steinweiss

Breakestra
Hit The Floor (Ubiquity Records, 2005)
Drums: Pete McNeal, Miles Tackett

The Pharcyde
Labcabincalifornia (Delicious Vinyl, 1995)
Production: Jay Dee a.k.a. J. Dilla, various

Lettuce
Rage! (Velour Recordings, 2008)
Drums: Adam Deitch

Galactic
From the Corner to the Block (Anti-, 2007)
Drums: Stanton Moore

The Roots
Things Fall Apart (MCA Records, 1999)
Drums: Ahmir "Questlove" Thompson

Marva Whitney
It's My Thing (King Records, 1969)
Drums: Clyde Stubblefield

Gang Starr
Moment of Truth (Noo Trybe Records, 1998)
Production: DJ Premier

Pretty Lights
Passing By Behind Your Eyes (2009)
Production: Derek Vincent Smith

Lyn Collins
Think (About It) (People, 1972)
Drums: John "Jabo" Starks

Heavy D and the Boyz
Big Tyme (MCA, 1989)
Production: DJ Eddie F, Heavy D, various

Duke Williams and the Extremes
Monkey in A Silk Suit Is Still A Monkey
(Capricorn, 1973)
Drums: Earl Young, Andy Newmark

Tower of Power
Back to Oakland (Warner Bros., 1974)
Drums: David Garibaldi

Digable Planets
Blowout Comb (Pendulum, 1994)
Production: Digable Planets

The Meters
Look-ka Py Py (Josie Records, 1969)
Drums: Joseph "Zigaboo" Modeliste

Kool and the Gang
Kool and the Gang (De-Lite, 1969)
Drums: George Brown

James Brown
In The Jungle Groove (Polydor, 1986)
Drums: Melvin Parker, Clyde
Stubblefield, John "Jabo" Starks

Big Daddy Kane
Prince of Darkness
(Cold Chillin, 1991)
Production: Big Daddy Kane,
Michael Warner

The Bamboos
Step It Up (Ubiquity, 2006)
Drums: Danny Farrugia

The Roots
How I Got Over (Def Jam, 2010)
Drums: Ahmir "Questlove" Thompson

Nas
It Was Written (Columbia, 1996)
Production: Poke and Tone, various

The Breakbeat Bible audio features select beats, exercises, and phrases from the book. Throughout the book, the exercises, beats, and phrases that appear on the audio are marked with the disc icon, along with their corresponding track number.

Also included are four play-along instrumental tracks created by the Paper.Beatz.Rock production team. These were built from loops of four randomly selected beats. *Instrumental #1* is based on a loop of track #84 (8th Element, Intro #5). *Instrumental #2* is based on a loop of track #136 (12th Element, Intro #3). *Instrumental #3* is based on chopped-up and rearranged pieces of track #124 (10th Element, 8-bar Phrase). *Instrumental #4* is based on a loop of track #71 (7th Element, Intro #2). There's also a bonus instrumental from Paper.Beatz.Rock, featuring drum programming by Remshot. The audio also includes *The Breakbeat Bible* sample library. This features 30 individual samples of the different drumset components, played at various velocities. You can use these to program your own drum patterns.

The instrumentals appear with and without drums. First, practice along to the instrumentals with drums. When practicing to the instrumentals without drums, you don't necessarily have to play the original drum pattern. You can use any exercise or beat from the book, or create your own. If you have trouble locking in with *Instrumental #2* (minus drums), keep counting and strengthening your internal clock—you'll eventually get it. Also, regarding *Instrumental #4* (minus drums), focus on locking in with the bass pattern. Don't let the keyboard part on the "and" of 4 throw you off. Think of *Instrumental #2* (track #166) and *Instrumental #4* (track #170) as extensions of the Click Track Loops.

About the Author

Mike Adamo was born in Morristown, NJ. He began playing drums at age eight and went on to study with Andy DeLuca, the great Joe Bergamini, Terry "Big T" Tanner, and Dan Mack. He's recorded and toured extensively as a founding member of the legendary band Mama's Cookin. The Cookin' has released three critically acclaimed albums: *House of Good Spirits*, *Let the Record Ride*, and *Mama's Cookin'*. After receiving a Bachelor of Arts degree in Sociology from Western State College of Colorado, he relocated to Lake Tahoe in order to hone his craft. Mike is currently based out of Oakland, CA. In addition to Mama's Cookin, he performs regularly with The Gravity Pimps, Lo-Fi 13, Ben Fuller, and The Funky Miracle, and has been teaching lessons for the past decade.

The Audio Track List

1. Intro. #1
2. Intro. #2
3. 1st Element Intro. #1
4. 1st Element Exercise #9
5. 1st Element Exercise #11
6. 1st Element Beat #4
7. 1st Element Beat #8
8. 1st Element 8-Bar Phrase
9. 2nd Element Intro. #1
10. 2nd Element Exercise #9
11. 2nd Element Exercise #10
12. 2nd Element Beat #2
13. 2nd Element Beat #9
14. 2nd Element 8-Bar Phrase
15. Elements 1 & 2 Review Phrase #1
16. Elements 1 & 2 Review Phrase #2
17. 3rd Element Intro. #1
18. 3rd Element Intro. #2
19. 3rd Element Intro. #3
20. 3rd Element Intro. #4
21. 3rd Element Intro. #5
22. 3rd Element Intro. #6
23. 3rd Element Intro. #7
24. 3rd Element Exercise #5 (mezzo forte)
25. 3rd Element Exercise #5 (ghosted)
26. 3rd Element Exercise #5 (control strokes)
27. 3rd Element Exercise #5 (pull outs)
28. 3rd Element Exercise #9 (mixed patterns)
29. 3rd Element Exercise #10 (mixed patterns)
30. 3rd Element Beat #6
31. 3rd Element Beat #9
32. 3rd Element 8-Bar Phrase
33. 4th Element Intro. #1
34. 4th Element Intro. #2
35. 4th Element Intro. #3
36. 4th Element Intro. #4
37. 4th Element Exercise #9
38. 4th Element Exercise #13
39. 4th Element Beat #2
40. 4th Element Beat #12
41. 4th Element 8-Bar Phrase
42. Elements 1-4 Review Phrase #1
43. Elements 1-4 Review Phrase #2

44. Elements 1-4 Review (bonus exercise #1)
45. Elements 1-4 Review (bonus exercise #2)
46. Elements 1-4 Review (bonus exercise #3)
47. Elements 1-4 Review (bonus exercise #4)
48. 5th Element Intro. #1
49. 5th Element Intro. #2
50. 5th Element Intro. #3
51. 5th Element Intro. #4
52. 5th Element Intro. #5
53. 5th Element Intro. #6
54. 5th Element Intro. #7
55. 5th Element Exercise #5
56. 5th Element Exercise #11
57. 5th Element Beat #6
58. 5th Element Beat #11
59. 5th Element 8-Bar Phrase
60. 6th Element Intro. #1
61. 6th Element Intro. #2
62. 6th Element Intro. #3
63. 6th Element Intro. #4
64. 6th Element Intro. #5
65. 6th Element Intro. #6
66. 6th Element Intro. #7
67. 6th Element Beat #7
68. 6th Element Beat #11
69. 6th Element 8-Bar Phrase
70. 7th Element Intro. #1
71. 7th Element Intro. #2
72. 7th Element Intro. #3
73. 7th Element Intro. #4
74. 7th Element Intro. #5
75. 7th Element Exercise #5
76. 7th Element Exercise #8
77. 7th Element Beat #2
78. 7th Element Beat #12
79. 7th Element 8-Bar Phrase
80. 8th Element Intro. #1
81. 8th Element Intro. #2
82. 8th Element Intro. #3
83. 8th Element Intro. #4
84. 8th Element Intro. #5

85. 8th Element Intro. #6
86. 8th Element Exercise #13
87. 8th Element Exercise #21
88. 8th Element Beat #4
89. 8th Element Beat #12
90. 8th Element 8-Bar Phrase
91. 9th Element Intro. #1
92. 9th Element Intro. #2
93. 9th Element Intro. #3
94. 9th Element Intro. #4
95. 9th Element Intro. #5
96. 9th Element Intro. #6
97. 9th Element Intro. #7
98. 9th Element Intro. #8
99. 9th Element Intro. #9
100. 9th Element Intro. #10
101. 9th Element Intro. #11
102. 9th Element Exercise #1 (mixed hi-hat patterns)
103. 9th Element Exercise #8 (mixed hi-hat patterns)
104. 9th Element Beat #3 (mixed hi-hat patterns)
105. 9th Element Beat #9 (mixed hi-hat patterns)
106. 9th Element Exercise #1 (mixed hi-hat patterns w/ ghosted snare notes)
107. 9th Element Exercise #6 (mixed hi-hat patterns w/ ghosted snare notes)
108. 9th Element Beat #3 (mixed hi-hat patterns w/ ghosted snare notes)
109. 9th Element Beat #12 (mixed hi-hat patterns w/ ghosted snare notes)
110. 9th Element Exercise #4 (mixed hi-hat/ snare patterns w/ alternating sticking)
111. 9th Element Exercise #8 (mixed hi-hat/ snare patterns w/ alternating sticking)
112. 9th Element Beat #2 (mixed hi-hat/ snare patterns w/ alternating sticking)
113. 9th Element Beat #12 (mixed hi-hat/ snare patterns w/ alternating sticking)
114. 9th Element 8-Bar Phrase #1
115. 9th Element 8-Bar Phrase #2
116. 10th Element Intro. #1
117. 10th Element Intro. #2
118. 10th Element Intro. #3
119. 10th Element Intro. #4

Acknowledgements

My family, especially Mom, Dad, Matt, Marc, all aunts, uncles, and cousins for their never-ending love, patience, and support. My friends for always providing a source of inspiration and positivity. My band: Zeb Early, Steve LaBella, Todd Holway, and Eric Matlock for putting up with me and never making me drive. Paul Oliphant for helping me work out some of the concepts for this book. Joe Bergamini and everyone at Hudson for believing in the project. Todd Bogart and John Greer for their support and belief in me and the band. Rich Collins, Willie Rose, and Nick Buford for their extreme patience in dealing with me on this project. Rem and Brod for the beats. Barry Simons for the legal advice. Big up to the MSP and affiliates, Gunny/C.B. party people, Tahoe crew, Bay Area crew, all the fans, all my drum teachers, Mr. C. for keepin' it real, Brenda Flemming for the knowledge, all the musicians past, present, and future for keepin' the vibe alive, anyone that's shown love and support along the way: you know who you are and I'm forever grateful. Most importantly, All That Is, and The Great Unmanifested that pervades it all.

Stay tuned to www.thebreakbeatbible.com for more transcriptions, video lessons, links, beats, merchandise, discussion forum, and more.